MONEY SKILLS

for

TEENS

MONEY SKILLS

for

TEENS

Building a Solid Financial Mindset,
Decoding Paychecks and Banking, and Leveling Up
Through Budgeting, Saving, and Investing

KAE STOKES

Disclaimer

The information provided in this book is for educational and informational purposes only. While every effort was used in preparing this book, the author and publisher make no representations or warranties concerning the accuracy or completeness of the content, expressly disclaim any implied warranties, and shall not be liable for losses of profit or damages, including but not limited to special, incidental, consequential, or personal. The advice and strategies contained herein may not suit every individual or situation, and readers should exercise judgment and consult with relevant professionals where appropriate.

Paperback ISBN: 9798877766662
Hardcover ISBN: 9798877847934

Dedication

To my half-dozen.

You are my brightest stars, and this book is dedicated to you with all my love. May the wisdom within these pages illuminate your path to a prosperous future. Your potential is limitless. Your dreams are worth pursuing. Embrace challenges, savor victories, and never forget your strength and brilliance.

Table of Contents

FREE BONUS

Thank you for purchasing my book! And here's a free bonus! To claim it, simply scan the QR Code or visit the URL below.

https://inkscribebooks.com/free-bonus

ZERO-BASED BUDGETING GUIDE
Toolkit for Effective Money Management

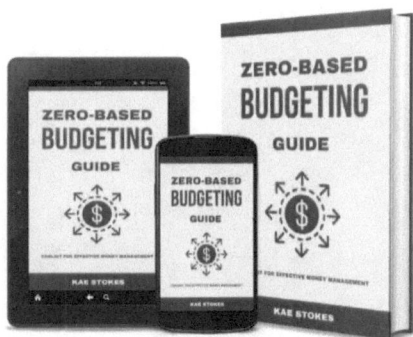

Effective money management is an ever-essential life skill for teens, and this guide gives you the tools needed to master it!

Claim your free bonus and discover how to maximize every dollar you earn. Take that first step toward financial success!

"It's never too early to learn money skills."

Introduction

Congratulations on reaching teenage status! You can now kick back with friends without your parents hovering, swing by the convenience store for snacks on your way to school, and hit the burger joint with your team after the big win. It's the sweetest taste of independence. But amidst the thrill of these carefree moments, do you also sense a whisper of change in the air? A feeling that soon, you'll be asked to step into bigger shoes?

Welcome to this unique in-between where you're savoring your newfound freedom one moment and feeling the weight of responsibilities creeping in the next. Your thoughts are transitioning from "Woohoo!" to "Wait a minute." You're realizing that those free lunch days are gradually coming to an end, and you're thinking about … money—not so much in the way of counting how much you have left for tomorrow's convenience store trip but in the way of managing those dollars and cents. In fancier terms, you're thinking about personal finances. This is a pivotal moment, and kudos to you! Your early awareness about money means you're off to an amazing start.

Let me take a shot at some guesses. You're between 13 and 18 years old. You've accepted the fact that your allowance won't cut it anymore. You're eager to learn about money, but nobody in your circle is really talking about it. You're thinking about getting a part-time job, and your mind is already buzzing about what to do with the money you'll earn. You're curious about how people become rich and are motivated to learn the ways. And now, you've decided to face responsibility head-on. You've discovered this book, and the title says it all—it encompasses everything you'd want to know about money. Did I hit the mark with my guesses? Kinda sorta? Not so? Eh—scratch all that. Your parents gave this book to you to read! Is that it? In any case, *I'm glad you're here.*

My friend—can I call you a friend? Money is a powerful tool. It can build your dreams or secure shackles around your ankles. With such extremes, why isn't money sufficiently taught in every high school? I don't mean math money; I mean personal finance money. How to manage your money, money.

Your school curriculum covers everything from calculus to the history of the world. Yet, it's lacking in one of the most crucial subjects you'll use all your life. Shocking! And your parents? They want you to succeed, and that's why this book is in your hands. It's just that sometimes, the hustle and bustle of life can get in the way, and as much as they sprinkle money lessons at you, providing you with a book can spark further interest and speed up the process—because they care.

The lack of personal finance education can leave many people stagnant in a world that's supposed to be filled with opportunities. So, let's fill this glaring gap together!

What if I told you that you could start building wealth while you're in high school, even with little money? What if I said you don't need to be a financial expert or have extensive tech know-how? And what if I assured you that it wouldn't demand a significant chunk of your time, allowing you to continue doing all your teenage things while letting that initial wealth take off on its own? By the time you graduate, you'll have scripted a chapter or two of your financial success story.

Well, you *can* start building wealth now, utilizing the skills you already have, all while continuing to experience the full spectrum of your teenage years—I'll show you how. Soon, you'll add even more chapters to your story. One day, as you read it back, you'll think, "I've come a long way." It may be difficult to see past your current bubble when the financial world can seem like a corn maze, but armed with the proper knowledge and guidance, you'll start seeing the possibilities beyond that bubble and navigate the maze like a pro.

Do you want to be rich? Maybe "rich" isn't the right word. Do you want to be financially free? To have the freedom to make choices without worrying about money? Do you have aspirations for your future and wonder how to turn them into reality? Do you envision a life filled with dignity rather than regret? I'll answer for you: YES! In that case, you know precisely what you must do: *learn personal finance.*

Let me be clear: It's your money and your future. No one—and I mean, no one—will care more about your money than you do. So, it's time to get your head out of the clouds, pause daydreaming, and get your mind geared up for some valuable money lessons! Don't shrug it off for later—because, as you and I know, later may never arrive.

Picture this: You land your first job, and suddenly, you're making money. It's five, seven, ten, or even twenty times your allowance (if you even had one). It's electrifying! But you're not used to all this money coming at you at once. It's no longer a five-dollar decision at the local convenience store. Naturally, you start to feel a little anxious. Not in an OMG stressful way but in the sense that you're now entering the realm of financial choices that carry more impact—the stakes are higher. It's like stepping into uncharted territories where each decision puts a stamp on the map that can't be erased and you're forced to think harder.

Now, a little anxiousness is a good thing. It's your body telling you to "fight or flight"—a biological signal to face a difficult situation head-on or run away. Oh, *you're* going to face it. *You're* going to learn how to manage your money. The truth is—earning money is instinctual, and spending it is a complete no-brainer. Managing it? Well, *this must be learned.*

Many adults haven't learned to manage their money, so why should you? And if you do, how will you do that? It's easy to get lost and stay lost when you follow those in the generation ahead of you who are struggling to get it together. But if you grasp the reins of personal finance and steer your own cart, you'll never have to worry about being lost—or broke. Ultimately, you can become a positive example for others in your generation and after, inspiring them to achieve similar financial success.

The consequences of neglecting financial education can be dire. You may go through life overspending, accumulating debt, and missing out on all sorts of opportunities to grow wealth. It's like trying to build a house without knowing how to lay the bricks—the foundation will be weak, and the entire structure may collapse. But when laid properly, that brick foundation can withstand the test of time, requiring only routine maintenance to ensure it remains stable.

The earlier you learn personal finance, the sooner you'll reap a chain reaction of benefits. Learning personal finance empowers you to take control of your money. This, in turn, helps you avoid financial traps that can leave you drowning in debt. By steering clear of debt, you can invest in self-improvement and lay the groundwork for building wealth. Ultimately, you'll become a skillful decision-maker in money management. All in all, these skills contribute to your excellence in every aspect of life: personal, academic, and career. And when you start seeing money through this lens, suddenly, "Money is power" means something much deeper, far more than what we give it credit for—it becomes your ticket to a well-crafted life. Quite the chain reaction.

OVERVIEW OF *MONEY SKILLS FOR TEENS*

Money Skills for Teens is your complete guide to personal finance. It will teach you how to manage your money, leverage its power to build wealth, and achieve the dream of financial freedom. What it won't teach you is how to get rich quick. Chasing after get-rich-quick schemes isn't sustainable. These schemes promise you fast and easy wealth but rarely deliver.

They prey on your emotions, creating a roller coaster of hope and disappointment, leaving you feeling more of a failure than anything else. You've heard of this before—if something seems too good to be true, it probably is. And when it comes to get-rich-quick schemes, the probability is higher. So, rather than chasing shortcuts that take longer or get you lost, let's concentrate on what managing money should be about— building foundations, acquiring skills, accumulating wealth, and achieving lasting success.

This book is for *you* (and my younger self)—that young, carefree person who "doesn't really" need to worry about money yet, except you do. It encapsulates everything I wish I had learned about money when I was your age—it's my one regret. I don't want you to experience that same regret; it's a hard pill to swallow. With a bright future ahead, I hope this book resonates with you, inspires you, and energizes you for what's to come.

I've simplified complex ideas into easily understood discussions. While certain sections may seem a bit dry, they're essential to your understanding of money. I won't overwhelm you with lengthy details I'm tempted to discuss. Still, I'll provide you with just the right amount of information to empower you and set you on the path to getting "rich." It's not a short path, but it's a simple one. However, it can be rough if you don't embark now.

Within these pages, you'll discover fundamental principles, key concepts, essential terminology, practical exercises, real-life examples, insightful comparisons, and valuable tips to enrich your financial journey.

First, we'll start with a comprehensive section on building a solid financial mindset. Don't skip this—it sets the stage for everything that follows. Next, we'll cover banking, employment, and paychecks. After that, we'll move on to budgeting, saving, and investing. Finally, we'll finish with credit cards and taxes.

Feel free to skim through particular sections of this book if you've strutted along a financial block or two. But don't skim too much. You're entering the personal finance world here, and it'll take more than a couple of blocks to circle all the way around—and you may miss out on some hidden insights.

Some examples may require you to put yourself in the position of an adult, so keep this in mind. Beyond that, embrace the journey of discovering the ins and outs of money management. Let's navigate this personal finance thing together and uncover the valuable lessons that will shape your financial future. I believe that if you open your heart to the core message of this book, it can be the catalyst that starts it all for you. Here's to your best. *And parents—thank you for investing in your teen's financial education.*

Before diving in, take a moment to reflect on these questions:

- How do you view money?
- What do you want to achieve with money?
- What would your life look like if you had all the financial resources you needed?

All set?

Excited?

Let's get started.

1

———∞———

Building a Solid Financial Mindset

You may think money is just about numbers, bank accounts, and dollar bills. I've got news for you. Money is more about what's going on in your head than what's in your wallet. Let's break it down and see why building a solid financial mindset is like laying the foundation for a skyscraper.

Picture two friends: One splurges every dollar they earn on the latest gadgets, trendy clothes, and dining out, while the other strategically saves, spends wisely, and thinks about long-term goals like buying a car or going to college. What sets them apart? It's their distinct view on money. The first sees it as merely a disposable resource. The second sees it as a way to craft a dream life—and *this* is the mindset you'll need to attain a future filled with achievements rather than stuff.

A financial mindset refers to your positive beliefs, attitudes, and behaviors about money. It's recognizing that money is a tool for shaping your future rather than a means for spending thoughtlessly. Mastering a solid financial mindset involves understanding money's value, spending wisely, setting priorities, resisting temptations, evaluating trade-offs, focusing on long-term goals, and cultivating self-awareness. Achieving this solid mindset is akin to mastering other skills, such as perfecting the violin or excelling in sports—it requires consistent practice and dedication. While it may seem like a long list to master, the end reward is the ability to live life on your own terms. We strive for this goal, so let's build a solid financial mindset together.

UNDERSTANDING THE VALUE OF MONEY

So you're craving Jamba Juice. A small smoothie will cost you roughly $7. It's easy to hand over that $7 without a second thought. It's hot outside; you're thirsty and want something quick and refreshing. At the moment, it makes perfect sense.

But remember those three questions you reflected on earlier, one being, "What do you want to achieve with money?" Let's crunch some numbers: $7 spent once is $7—no big deal. $7 spent five days a week is a whopping $1,820 a year. Think of everything you can do with $1,820 if you forgo your daily

Jamba. Or, even if you ease up a bit and slash it in half, you'd still save $910. Can you think of other possibilities for that cash? I can. It's incredible how small changes can lead to significant savings and open up new opportunities.

Understanding the value of money means recognizing *what else* your money can do for you. It's not just fixed dollars and cents; its worth can change depending on what you want, what you need, and how you decide to use it. So, how can you make thoughtful choices about your money?

Think Before You Spend

Think a bit harder before heading out for that smoothie. Is it truly what you want right now? Consider *what else* that $7 could do for you. Perhaps you're saving for something more substantial, like a mountain bike. How will this $7 purchase impact your larger goal? While giving up that daily smoothie for a bike may seem challenging initially, recognize that habits work in reverse. By consciously skipping it just once, then again—and again, soon, you'll find yourself no longer craving that weekly indulgence as much but only stopping in every now and then. Eventually, thinking before you spend becomes the *new* habit, and every $7 saved is another $7 toward a new bike. Imagine the satisfaction of taking home that new bike after consciously stacking up all those forgone $7s. Or should I say, "lucky $7s." So now, every time you stack a $7, think of it as increasing your luck.

Recognize Money's True Worth

Understand money's true worth. It's more than what meets the eye and goes beyond its face value. While a solo $7 may seem insignificant, its weight accumulates over time. Saving $7 every week can result in a solid $364 in a year. $364 worth of weekly smoothies purchased out of sheer habit may not capture its true worth, but redirecting those individual $7s can. An upgraded guitar, a ski trip with friends, or a leap toward something you've always wanted can represent the true worth of those dollars once accumulated. And don't brush off that $7 smoothie you got on that scorching day—it may be worth every penny.

We're not cutting out all Jamba trips; we're just pulling out one. You can still have your other four fixes during the week while stacking up $364 for whatever floats your boat. Try skipping it twice a week—what's worth $728? Amp it up to three times, and now you're looking at $1,092. Feeling the shift? The more you see these numbers increase, the less those smoothie cravings kick in. It's about recognizing the value of your choices and witnessing your money's potential unfold right before your eyes.

Spend on What Matters

Align your spending with what holds greater importance to you. If you have a passion for art, saving that $7 toward a quality set of painting supplies may be a thoughtful choice, especially if you're buying that smoothie only because your friends wanted to stop in and you're just going along. If you value fitness and healthy eating and don't spend regularly on other things, a $7 daily treat at Jamba Juice is a sensible purchase. *It's mindfulness over dollars.*

The next time you're craving a blended fruit smoothie, take a moment to think about the bigger picture and what that $7 can become. Sure, it's only Jamba Juice today, but those few dollars can become a surmountable amount of money over time. Whether it's saving for a new cool gadget or a passion project, your money has the power to achieve extraordinary things—you just need to give it a chance to serve a purpose beyond immediate spending. Your wallet isn't just a holder of cash; it's a key to the future shaped by intentional choices. Thinking before spending, recognizing money's true worth, and spending on what matters aren't mere words; they can get you access to the key.

This type of talk may sound heavy for the first chapter, but bear with me. Spending money may seem like just a few dollars tossed around here and there, but believe it or not, those decisions can truly define your life. Even at this age, understanding this "heavy" talk sets you on a path to becoming a pro at handling your finances. Stick around, and we'll jump into more practical tips and real-life scenarios just as insightful to make this money journey engaging.

Practical Exercise: The $7 Challenge

For one week, keep track of every $7 you spend. When the week is up, look back and ask yourself: Were those purchases worth it? Did they align with my values? Did I enjoy them? This exercise gives you a clear picture of where your money is going. It helps you evaluate whether it's heading in the direction it needs to go.

DISTINGUISHING WISE VS. UNWISE SPENDING

You're probably starting to spend more money. Deep down, you *know* you should spend wisely because no one ever encourages wasteful spending. However, we sometimes spend money too quickly without thinking about its impact. It's essential to bring that existing inner awareness to the surface and consciously battle it out with yourself when distinguishing between wise and unwise spending. This way, you spend money purposefully and avoid the consequences of wasteful spending, such as not having anything left over to cover your necessities as the month progresses or to rescue yourself from a sticky situation that came out of nowhere.

Wise spending involves purchasing things you genuinely need or those that significantly improve your life or the lives of others. Buying a new pair of tennis shoes to replace your worn-out ones, investing in study guides to ace your exams, or dedicating your savings to a thoughtful Mother's Day gift to show your love and appreciation (I'm grinning) are examples of wise spending.

On the other hand, unwise spending occurs when you buy things you neither need nor genuinely want. It often involves making impulse purchases, whether due to items being on sale or because your friends have them—or it could be out of utter boredom. Unfortunately, frequent unwise spending can lead to a thin wallet, stress, and regret. It's important to recognize that money is more than pocket change; it represents opportunities waiting for those willing and ready to harness its potential. By taking your finances seriously and breaking the habit of unwise spending, you'll see those opportunities emerge and appreciate the impact of each wise spending decision; each one makes a difference.

Distinguishing between wise and unwise spending may appear straightforward because it only requires basic math. However, it's a matter of psychology rather than intelligence. Suppose you only have $25 left before payday, but the item you want to buy costs $100. You whip out your credit card to pay for it. You *know* you can't afford it, but that doesn't hold you back. Your mind subconsciously justifies your decision with, "Why not buy it if you *can*?" but neglects to consider the consequences of racking up unpaid credit card debt. You convince yourself that you'll have the money to pay the debt.

Letting loose with spending because you "can" could get you into trouble down the road. Often, all it takes is a few seconds of contemplation to kick an impulse to the curb. Keep this tip in your head, and tap the brakes the next time you're about to splurge on an item four times the amount you have. Pause for that seesaw moment and weigh the short-term satisfaction against the long-term consequences—is that momentary thrill worth the lasting headache? Quickly think: Is it *wise* to spend on something when you don't have the cash at the time to pay for it? Is it *wise* to accumulate debt you likely can't pay off just to take that item home today? Or is it *wise* to wait until you have the $100 cash? Or even just wait? These few seconds may save you.

Practical Exercise: Use Cash

Debit cards and credit cards make spending effortless. You swipe your card, claim your purchase, and get your card *back*. Psychologically, you haven't given up anything, so there's no pain involved. When you hand over your Benjamin, it's a different story—it's gone for good, and it hurts. Use cash; it makes you think twice and hard.

IDENTIFYING NEEDS VS. WANTS

There's a fine line that separates two fundamental principles: needs vs. wants; our money decisions hover around this line.

You may think it's a topic so elementary that even your little sibling could explain the difference to you. Yet, many of us struggle with this basic concept. Even if you already "get it," talking about it can help reinforce the idea, enabling you to maneuver the winding landscape of your money decisions. Because, let's face it, the internet has a way of flashing stuff at us, and the clear line between needs and wants can sometimes blur. Identifying this line sharpens the distinction and provides a gentle nudge toward making wiser spending decisions, even if it's not a need.

Needs are the must-haves. They're the essential items and elements required for basic human survival and well-being, making them crucial for a comfortable life. Needs include food, water, shelter, clothing, sanitation, transportation, and healthcare. Without these, daily life can become a constant struggle. Needs *always* come first, serving as the foundation for security and peace of mind.

Wants are the nice-to-haves. They're the extras that enhance your life by adding enjoyment, luxury, or convenience, but they aren't essential for survival. They make you feel good or look good, but not much else. These include the latest tech gadgets, designer clothing, fashionable accessories, fine dining, luxury cars, spa treatments, and dream vacations. The allure of it all makes it easy to overlook the financial impact. Spending on wants is okay, but *only* after caring for needs.

Finding the optimal balance between spending on needs and wants can help you manage your money effectively. Think of it like dieting. Just as it's easier to stick to a diet that doesn't eliminate all your favorite foods, you're more likely to succeed in controlling your spending when you leave room for some wants here and there.

Needs vs. wants may seem obvious, but what appears obvious often doesn't align with reality when it comes to spending money. It's easy to talk your way into it and get carried away with expenses that may appear necessary but are actually wants. Therefore, developing a clear understanding of the distinction between needs and wants and being open to receiving reinforcement helps you prioritize essentials and enjoy luxuries *only* when your basic needs are met. This fundamental concept is at the heart of effective money management, ensuring your financial foundation remains solid.

So, the next time you find yourself at the crossroads of spending, let this simple mantra echo in your thoughts: *needs first, wants second*. You're laying the groundwork for a comfortable life while adding the spice and flair that is uniquely yours. You'll have plenty of opportunities to infuse this extra spice and flair into your life, so there's no need to go "all in" on wants. It's hard to mess up your finances when you follow that mantra, even if you follow it less than perfectly. So needs first; sprinkle in wants after.

19

PRACTICING DELAYED GRATIFICATION

We live in a world that screams, "Buy now, think later!" It's in the ads on your phone, the commercials on your favorite show, and those enticing sale signs at the mall. Waiting isn't easy when you've got money in your pocket, and something shiny and new is calling your name. That game on a 20% sale for $50 may seem too good to pass, especially when a bright red sign displays "Limited Time Only." But what about those new track shoes you'll *need* in a few months? Here's where the principle of delayed gratification comes in.

Waiting Patiently

Delayed gratification is about the art of waiting patiently—a skill integral to resisting the temptation of immediate pleasures in favor of achieving more significant, long-term goals. It doesn't mean completely denying yourself fun or never spending money on the things you like. Instead, it's about gaining the discipline to say *no* to the latest and greatest items on the store shelf so you can say *yes* to your future car. This skill requires setting priorities and thoughtful planning, and it goes hand in hand with responsible money management. Although these abilities don't come naturally, with practice, patience, and mindfulness, you can acquire them and ultimately enjoy the rewards of your future choices. The allure of the latest and greatest or the promise of a future car— which will you choose?

Preventing Buyer's Remorse

You know the feeling. You see something you like, and you want it now. Maybe it's a new bag or a pair of shoes. Before you know it, your wallet is lighter, and you may feel an uneasy twinge of regret. That's the trap of impulse buying—the sneaky villain in this story that's everywhere, like on your social feed, loaded with all kinds of people flaunting their latest purchases, from the new and improved to the best of the best to the state of the art. You may get hooked good, staring at it long enough; there's something for everyone. As if getting hooked once wasn't painful enough, you circle back for another bite, giving the villain exactly what it wants.

We've all been there, giving in to the immediate want. But when the temptation strikes, remind yourself of the power of delayed gratification. Pause, talk yourself through it, and ask the critical question: *Is this truly a need or a want?* Resisting the impulse and walking away may feel like a tug-a-war in the heat of the moment, but it needs to happen.

While the initial thrill of an impulse purchase can be exhilarating, it's usually short-lived, leaving you with the dreaded buyer's remorse—a soaring high swiftly followed by a disheartening low. You'll end up hitting your hand against your head for not thinking things through and wishing you hadn't made the ridiculous purchase. "What was I thinking?" is the typical dilemma here.

Honing in on delayed gratification as soon as the tug-a-war begins can keep you on the winning side, freeing you from the side of grief and regret. Understanding delayed gratification acts as your shield against buyer's remorse. So, put this skill to work each time you're tugging at yourself in the middle of the store aisle so that by the end of it, you can say, "I'm glad I made the right choice."

Avoiding the Struggles of Debt

Back to those people on your social feed flaunting their latest buys—what you don't see is their struggle with credit card debt. Many people fall into an unending cycle of credit card debt because they seek immediate enjoyment without thinking about long-term consequences. It's too easy to get caught in the suction cup of instant gratification living in a society that encourages impulsive spending. However, delayed gratification helps you avoid that struggle by instilling the discipline to save and patiently wait until you can afford the things you want. When you've diligently saved up, the sense of accomplishment is incomparable to the passing thrill of instant gratification. Even more so, you've avoided the web of debt that has trapped those who once flaunted their stuff. Instead, you've taken a proud step closer to financial success.

Focusing on Long-Term Goals

When you decide to save that $50 toward buying those track shoes *later* instead of giving it all up for that game right now, you're prioritizing what truly matters and making a choice that reflects your commitment to long-term goals. It may be a minor decision, but it reflects a big-picture approach to managing your finances and your life.

Imagine a 1,000-piece jigsaw puzzle, with each piece symbolizing a $50 savings goal. Every time you save an additional $50, it's like adding another piece to the puzzle, gradually bringing the image into clear view. By delaying gratification by $50 each time you're presented with a temptation, you're connecting another puzzle piece toward attaining your long-term goal. The final piece screams victory—"Yes! I did it!"

Building Better Habits

Practicing delayed gratification helps you form the habit of careful spending. As you choose to delay immediate satisfaction, weighing all your options, you're actively considering your needs and matching your spending decisions with your values and goals. Over time, this habit of mindful spending extends beyond your finances; you'll develop an innate sense of intentionality and purpose in everything you do. As a result, life becomes less stressful because you're not scrambling to reverse hasty mishaps.

Nailing It

Mastering the art of delayed gratification is a skill that goes beyond its principle; it requires deliberate practice. Though resisting the temptations to prioritize long-term goals may seem challenging, the ultimate achievement of those goals makes every difficult situation worth it in hindsight.

Here are some tips to help you nail the art of delayed gratification and reap the rewards of patience and discipline:

- Ask Yourself: Is this a want or a need? Do I need this now? What will I gain by waiting? What else could this money do for me? Do I even have the cash for it? How am I feeling? Will I regret it later? These questions can filter impulsive motivations and provide clarity.

- Make Your Goals Tangible: Identify your savings goals; write them down neatly and purposefully. Keep them visible to remind yourself of their significance. Having goals that can be seen and touched can make it easier to fight those sneak attacks.

- Wait 48 Hours: When faced with the temptation of an impulse purchase, wait 48 hours and use the time to think it over. More often than not, the initial urge to spend will pass, providing you with a sense of accomplishment and reinforcing your self-control.

- Seek an Alternative: If you're tempted to splurge on a particular item, look for a lower-cost or no-cost alternative that satisfies the itch without derailing your plans.

- Reward Yourself Along the Way: Break up your larger goals into smaller milestones and treat yourself when you reach them. Enjoying small rewards while keeping an eye on the larger goal can supply an emotional boost, preventing you from caving in at the worst moment.

Good things often take time. Patiently waiting, intentionally saving, and actively working toward what you genuinely want can make the reward sweeter. It's not so much about those new track shoes as it is about the satisfaction of achieving something you set your mind to and worked hard for. Delayed gratification is the ultimate financial power tool that helps you drill down on your decisions, take control of your emotions and money, and move steadily toward your goals.

RECOGNIZING OPPORTUNITY COST

Opportunity cost may sound like one of those dry terms that only economists get excited about. But trust me, once you understand what it means, it'll blow your mind and excite you, too. It's like unlocking a secret superpower that can turbocharge your money decisions.

Opportunity cost is all about choices. It's the value of what you're passing up—the next best thing—whenever you make a decision. It involves trading time, energy, and potential for one thing over another (Fernando, 2023). Let's use a concrete example to make it crystal clear. Yes, concrete is not crystal clear, but this example is.

Imagine this scenario: You have $700 monthly to pay for a car. You've done your research and narrowed your choices to two cars. One would set you back the entire $700 a month, and the other, $500 a month. You ultimately go with the $700 car. You didn't go over, and that's great. But not so fast.

What if you had chosen the cheaper car? It's not as flashy and doesn't have keyless entry or a backup camera, but it would still get you to school or work and back. Now, here's where things get interesting. What if you took the $200 difference between the two car payments and invested it instead? Assuming your investment returns you 10% over five years—the typical length of a car loan—your $200 saved monthly would grow to $14,974.34 (Investor.gov, n.d.). *That's the opportunity cost* of going with the pricier, flashier car! This 10% will be explained later when we discuss investing.

And news alert! Cars depreciate—meaning they lose value over time, and for cars, it happens fast. So, not only did you miss out on almost $15,000 in potential earnings, but your car might be begging for a replacement. Talk about adding salt to an open wound. Beating a dead horse. Putting fuel on the fire. Can you think of another one? Oh! Pouring money into a sinking ship. Throwing good money after bad. Adding insult to injury. Ok, I'll stop there. But do you see what I mean?

The point is to recognize what you're giving up. Sure, that flashier car may boost your self-esteem, but here's the real deal (and this is a recurring notion): Every financial choice you make today, no matter how small, carries the power to influence your financial future. What if everything comes attached with an Opportunity Cost label?

When you wrap your head around the idea of opportunity cost, it's like a light bulb flickering to life. You start seeing things from a whole new perspective, as if looking through a crystal ball that reveals the hidden costs and benefits behind every financial decision. You begin to *value* each dollar beyond its immediate use. You become *aware* that every choice has a trade-off. You now *think* about your money's long-term potential and naturally ask, "*What else* could this money do for me?" Essentially, every difficult decision becomes an element in the future you're crafting. Craft it well.

Practical Exercise: Create a Wish List
List some things you want to buy or save for, along with their costs. Next to each item, carefully consider what you'll have to give up or adjust in order to get it. Doing this helps you understand the trade-offs involved and make intelligent decisions about your money.

FOCUSING ON SMART GOALS

A solid financial mindset is intricately connected with goal setting. Goals aren't wishes. There's a big difference between wishing for something and establishing a plan to achieve it. Wishing is passive—it's hoping something will fall into your lap. On the other hand, goals demand your action. You need to formulate a plan, take charge, stay focused, go through the steps, and follow through to the end.

In the realm of personal finance, goal setting must also be concise. For instance, "My goal is to save more money" lacks precision. While it's a commendable goal, nothing can set it in motion. However, transforming it into a SMART goal can. A SMART goal is Specific, Measurable, Achievable, Relevant, and Time-Bound (Herrity, 2023). Applying these criteria to your financial goals will enhance your chances of achieving them. The setup is just as important as the goal. When the setup isn't SMART, you may fall short of your goal, leading to frustration and the temptation to quit.

Now, let's take apart each component of the SMART framework and create a concise, actionable plan:

- Specific: "I want to buy a new mountain bike. I'm preparing for a mountain bike event seven months away. My current bike is in poor condition."

- Measurable: "The least expensive mountain bike that suits my needs costs $1,200, including taxes. There's a pricier model at $1,500, which I'm willing to consider if I can save more. I'll monitor my progress monthly."

- Achievable: "I can save $200 monthly from my part-time job, which still leaves me enough money for daily spending. I'll ask my boss to give me additional hours if necessary to accelerate my savings. If that's not possible, I'll keep daily spending low."

- Relevant: "Mountain biking is more than just a hobby; it helps me stay active and connects me with a close-knit community of enthusiasts. This upcoming event is rare, and I want to ensure I have a mountain bike that won't hinder my performance."

- Time-Bound: "I want to purchase the mountain bike in six months, or five months if I can get additional working hours."

With your SMART goal defined, your *want* transforms from a random thought into an inspirational *plan*. This specific, measurable, achievable, relevant, and time-bound goal has meaning and purpose. It helps guide how you approach the process. You know that blowing all your cash on repeatedly going out to eat with friends won't get you closer to that bike, but putting in extra hours will. By documenting your goals in this structured manner, you're more likely to stay on top of your game because you're the sole player and the one accountable for the outcome. *It starts with you and ends with you.* No one else can define, chart, and bring your dreams to life but yourself. So, how badly do you want it?

Life is unpredictable, and situations can change unexpectedly. As you set out to achieve your dreams, remember that it's perfectly okay for your goals to have some flexibility. It allows you to adjust your plans in response to new information, opportunities, and challenges without feeling like you've failed. While reflecting on what holds great significance to you and creating a plan to achieve it, also anticipate possible setbacks. This way, you're equipped with the alternatives to keep pushing forward instead of giving up—one step back, two strides forward.

HANDLING MONEY AND PEER PRESSURE

Peer pressure. It's that nagging feeling that pushes you to do something just because everyone else is doing it. It's the voice in your head that says, "Come on, it'll be fun!"—even when you know it's not the best choice for you. It's that invisible force that sometimes makes you feel like you must act, dress, or look a certain way to fit in. Peer pressure isn't always like that; it can inspire you to seek new interests or excel in school.

However, there are instances when peer pressure can lead you down a path you don't want to go, especially when it comes to spending money. It has an easy way of sneaking into your financial life, whether it's the pressure to buy the latest devices, wear specific brands, or hang out frequently — "hang out" as in "spend money."

Imagine a Friday at the mall hanging out with your friends. Your initial plan was simple: meet up, goof around, and enjoy the experience with no intention of shopping. Your parents gave you $20, expecting that you would spend it on your usual mall treats—a pretzel and smoothie, things you typically enjoy when you go to the mall with them.

As you walk the mall, your friends shop for new clothes and gadgets. You're just tagging along, as you don't have money for shopping. Your group is now at the Nike store, and the clearance rack has suddenly grabbed your attention. In a moment of weakness, you bought a graphic tee, even though your $20 was meant for that usual pretzel and smoothie.

What made you buy the shirt? It wasn't because it was a rare graphic or a fantastic deal. It was the overwhelming pressure to fit in and not be the odd one out, especially when you stumbled on an item you could afford. In that instant, you felt a sense of relief, like you were finally part of the group. This pressure and relief, my friend, is peer pressure in action.

Although it may seem insignificant in the grand scheme of things, your choice was influenced by external factors rather than your conscious decision. In all of its various forms, peer pressure can be challenging enough. Financial peer pressure adds another layer of complexity, making it feel like you're balancing a tightrope (visualize this) between your plans and the expectations of those around you.

Your friends didn't push you to buy the graphic tee; you just felt pushed, as the decision to go with the tension may seem easier than going against it. It's essential to recognize that peer pressure doesn't always have to be obvious or come from pushy and insensitive friends. However, continuously feeling as if you must conform to whatever your well-meaning friends are up to can eventually lead to a sense of insecurity as you struggle to keep up. It's crucial to remember that your self-worth is not determined by what you own, wear, or look like. Your actions and attitude define it.

Financial peer pressure is inevitable, and yielding to it can substantially impact your financial well-being. However, becoming familiar with the signs of peer pressure can help you counteract its effects. Experiencing discomfort in certain situations, going against your principles, engaging in constant comparisons, feeling the need to keep up, and fighting stress after making a decision are all red flags that financial peer pressure may be at play.

When you identify any of these signs, recognize that you may be dealing with peer pressure, resist the urge to conform, and refrain from justifying your decisions or making excuses. Financial well-being takes priority, and staying true to your principles matters more than meeting external expectations.

A fundamental principle in handling peer pressure is self-awareness. The more attuned you are to your values, beliefs, interests, and boundaries, the better equipped you become to make financial decisions that serve your best interests and less likely to be swayed by popular opinion. So, invest time in deeply understanding yourself—who you are and all you stand for. This heightened self-awareness makes it easier to notice when peer pressure is at play. Trusting your instincts, raising those red flags, and confidently stepping back start to become second nature. Developing this ability strengthens the resilient financial mindset you're striving for.

Imagine a scenario where your friends excitedly share their Christmas gifts upon returning to school after the break. You only listen in, having received nothing "special." Feeling left out, you may be tempted to seek validation by asking your parents for a similar item, even though what your friends shared aren't things that typically interest you. Recognizing the discomfort as peer pressure, choosing not to dwell on it, and moving past the urge to conform empowers you to stay true to your authentic interests and values.

Peer pressure, while inevitable and whether subtle or blatant, can quickly derail your financial goals. Therefore, be mindful of it and stick to your principles—this way, you define your worth based on *your terms*, not anyone else's.

Tip: Be Assertive

Don't be afraid to tell your friends if something doesn't fit your budget (or your parents'). It's more than okay to give an assertive, "No, I can't," or suggest an affordable alternative. Your true friends will understand and respect your decisions—and your parents will be proud of your advocation.

2

---·∞·---

Stepping Into Banking

B anking encompasses various financial products and services designed to help you manage your money, including checking and savings accounts, credit cards, loans, mortgages, and safe deposit boxes. Our focus is checking and savings accounts—these act as your financial command centers, the hub from which all your saving, spending, and investing activities originate.

Checking and savings accounts are deposit accounts that offer a secure place to safeguard your money while providing the convenience of accessing your funds for various needs and time-frames. As a standard practice, these accounts are backed by government insurance programs, which ensures your money—typically up to $250,000—remains safe, in case your bank faces financial difficulties (Goldberg, 2023). It's a large amount, so don't worry about losing your savings. You can even store other $250,000s at multiple government-insured banks and every dollar would be safe, too (Goldberg, 2023). But that's a lot of money to keep idle. Unless you have immediate plans for such large funds, like buying a house, it's wise to invest a nice chunk of that. You'll learn later the importance of not keeping excess money idle.

Checking accounts offer versatility, providing quick and unrestricted access to your funds as the go-to source for everyday spending needs and routine transactions. They offer services and products such as direct deposits, wire transfers, ATMs, debit cards, and checks. Direct deposits allow payments to be received directly into your account, while wire transfers enable electronic fund movement between different accounts. ATMs grant instant access to your cash, and debit cards provide a convenient electronic means for making payments to individuals and businesses. Checks are an alternative payment method to debit cards and serve as a backup.

In contrast, savings accounts offer stability, allowing you to accumulate funds for your longer-term needs and helping you achieve your future financial goals. As an incentive to save, savings accounts provide more interest on your deposited funds than checking accounts and limit certain activities. For example, they restrict the number of withdrawals and outgoing transfers you can make each month, encouraging you to maintain a consistent inflow of funds rather than an outflow. Some savings accounts may require maintaining a minimum balance (Walrack, 2023).

The distinctive features of checking and savings accounts are both essential components in effective money management. While checking accounts offer the flexibility and accessibility required for day-to-day financial transactions, savings accounts provide the stability and growth potential necessary to reach your short-term and long-term goals. So, whether you're paying monthly bills, making daily purchases, or saving for a rainy day or a significant life milestone, these two accounts work together to help you manage your financial tasks and achieve your goals.

OPENING CHECKING AND SAVINGS ACCOUNTS

Opening checking and savings accounts is the first step in taking control of your finances. If you're not yet 18, you'll need the assistance of a parent or legal guardian to open the accounts; they will act as a joint owner for as long as you're under 18. They will accompany you, lead the conversation, complete and sign the bank documents, and make a small deposit as needed. If you're 18, you can handle this account opening process independently.

Many banks and credit unions provide dedicated teen accounts tailored to teen's limited needs and responsibilities. These accounts often include parental access and controls, along with features like no minimum deposit requirements and low or no associated fees (Rosenberg, 2023).

Credit unions present an alternative to the more familiar traditional banks like Bank of America or Wells Fargo, but they differ in structure. While banks operate for profit, credit unions are non-profit organizations and member-owned. This member-owned structure allows credit unions to prioritize serving their members by offering benefits such as higher interest on checking and savings accounts, lower fees and minimum balance requirements, and personalized customer service (Stevens, 2023). The unmatched benefits make credit unions a sensible choice for opening your first bank accounts. Therefore, don't limit your selection to traditional banks.

Opening teen checking and savings accounts is straightforward, especially if you choose a bank or credit union where your parents already have accounts. You'll need your ID and social security number to complete the application. These accounts can be opened online or at a branch location, and it's typical to achieve same-day activation. Once activated, you'll likely receive offers to sign up for online banking and download banking apps—consider taking advantage of these options. You'll receive a separate login and password from your co-owner. Your debit card will arrive by mail, and you can activate it by calling the number on the card—don't forget to sign the back of it. Finally, checks are typically not offered for teen accounts.

With your teen checking and savings accounts now active, you must proactively and diligently monitor your everyday activities to stay on top of your finances. Seemingly insignificant, $5 spent here and $10 spent there can quickly add up, and before you know it, you've depleted your account, and you're now waiting for more money to come in. Living paycheck to paycheck is a pattern you must avoid; it gives you zero chance at financial freedom.

Nowadays, tracking your money's comings and goings is incredibly easy. When you open your YouTube app, click on your bank app. Log in and check your balance and spending habits; it takes less than a minute. If you notice that you've visited Jamba Juice five times in three days, you may want to skip it for a couple of days. The simple act of checking makes you instantly more mindful. And it's quick.

This awareness will help you effectively oversee your accounts, take charge of your money, and steer your financial journey with confidence and responsibility. Be the big boss of your bank accounts—be the big boss of your future. None of this paycheck-to-paycheck stuff.

BREAKING DOWN A BANK STATEMENT

You've successfully made your mark in the banking world. Like clockwork, you'll begin receiving regular bank statements in your email or through snail mail. While these documents may not be the most captivating to read, it's essential to at least skim through the main items. We'll cover them in this section. We'll run through it quickly, sparing you from that "ugh" feeling that could come with what may appear like another boring class assignment so you don't start yawning and ditch the book. We've only just begun! However, if you're curious and would like to dissect a bank statement, ask your parents if you can check out one of theirs.

A bank statement is a monthly report from your bank summarizing your money's activities. It captures a snapshot of your Jamba Juice runs, snack refills, quick eats, mall hangouts, and store refunds (like that $20 graphic tee you bought at Nike out of weakness). Ideally, you should already know where your money went before receiving the bank statement, so the activities you see shouldn't be a surprise; you're now looking to find anything questionable.

Here's a quick run-down of the main items you'll see:

- Account Information: Your name, address, and account number.

- Statement Period: The timeframe covering your transactions.

- Beginning Balance: The amount in your account at the beginning of the statement period.

- Ending Balance: The amount in your account at the end of the statement period.

- Deposits and Credits: All money coming into your account, such as paychecks, incoming transfers, interest earned, and merchandise refunds.

- Withdrawals and Debits: All money leaving your account, such as ATM withdrawals, debit card purchases, cleared checks, and bill payments.

- Interest Earned: A small bonus for keeping money in your savings account and, depending on the institution, in your checking account.

- Fees: ATM fees, maintenance fees, overdraft fees, wire transfer fees, or other fees your bank may charge.

- Transaction Details: A list of your financial activities, showing dates, descriptions, merchants, amounts, and transaction types.

That's it—the main items skimmed. We breezed through that quickly (because any slower, and I may have lost you), but it's important to know that a bank statement is your monthly wake-up call. It offers insights into how well you handle your money, like the charge for that spur-of-the-moment movie with friends or that pair of designer jeans you bought on impulse and later returned. Seeing transactions listed on paper as solid proof that you did these things may prompt you to dial it down. It's like your friends calling you out on something, and you know it. Your friends keep you straight. Your bank statement can keep you straight.

Take a few moments each month to review your bank statement carefully to ensure everything adds up, literally and figuratively. If you ever find yourself scratching your head over a particular transaction, don't hesitate to contact your bank's customer service to help you unravel the mysteries of your money trail.

USING DEBIT CARDS AND ATMs

Debit cards and ATMs (automatic teller machines) offer incredible convenience. With a quick swipe of your plastic card and a few quick taps on the keypad, you can instantly access your cash through an ATM, eliminating the need to carry around wads of bills in your wallet. However, as convenient as debit cards and ATMs are, you should remember a few essential things when using them:

- Memorize Your PIN: A four-digit code, your Personal Identification Number (PIN), is your key to accessing the ATM and using your debit card. Memorize it and keep it confidential.

- Track Your Spending: When you use your debit card, money is instantly deducted from your bank account. While you're conscious of this process, the speed and seamlessness can lead to underestimating how quickly your funds deplete. Therefore, it's good to maintain a mental record of your account balance after each swipe and double-check it using your bank's mobile app.

- Use In-Network ATMs: Banks have a network of ATMs that offer free access to your money. You may incur fees if you go outside of the network (Smith, 2023). Know where your bank's in-network ATMs are in your area and make those your go-to locations to avoid unnecessary charges.

- Swipe With Sense: Having a debit card can make spending money way too fast and easy. Before swiping it, ask yourself: Why do I want this? Do I need this? Can I afford this? Is this worth it?

- Guard Your Card: Treat your debit card like you would cash. After you swipe, tuck it back into your wallet right away. If you can't find your debit card, call your bank to report it missing instead of hoping you'll soon find it.

By following these simple guidelines, you can easily access your money and make convenient transactions offered by debit cards and ATMs while reducing the chances of running into any issues.

Practical Exercise: A Week Without Swiping

Spend a week without swiping your debit card. Use cash and record your spending. When the week's up, reflect. Did it change how you spent your money? Did you think more about your purchases? This exercise can shed light on the downsides of solely using debit cards for your spending.

3

———— ∞ ————

Making Hard-Earned Money

Welcome to the world of making money, where you can realize your financial goals *and* develop invaluable life skills. Whether you're determined to save up for a particular purchase, acquire essential work experience, or refine your financial responsibility, there are two primary avenues teenagers can earn money: part-time jobs and freelancing.

STARTING A PART-TIME JOB

Starting a part-time job is your stepping stone into the world of work and will likely be your first taste of money; it's where you learn the ropes. This section will discuss finding and applying for part-time jobs tailored to your interests and skills.

Know the Laws

Before hopping off to find a job, familiarize yourself with the general laws governing teenage employment in your area. There may be specific restrictions on the hours you can work, the types of tasks you can perform, or even a requirement for a work permit.

Your school's district office is an excellent place to start, as they are typically responsible for issuing work permits. They should be your go-to resource for information related to teenagers seeking employment. They can provide the necessary documents, explain the legal requirements, and answer any questions about the process.

Tips for Seeking Your First Job

When it's time to seek your first job, align your interests and skills with potential opportunities. If you're passionate about animals, consider working at a local pet store or a dog-walking service. A retail or restaurant job may be an excellent fit if you excel in interpersonal skills. If you're exceptional at organizing, check out office clerk positions. And if you're an advanced swimmer, working as a lifeguard at your local community pool can be a rewarding option.

Don't forget the practical aspects of pay and proximity. As you explore various job opportunities, look for positions that not only align with your interests and skills but also offer reasonable compensation and are located nearby. When juggling school and work, you want to make the best use of your valuable time, so it's nice to get to work fast. This combination can make your first part-time job experience enjoyable, financially rewarding, and time-efficient. The grocery store within walking distance from home can fit the bill perfectly. Not only that, grocery stores often hire teens—an easy hire.

Crafting Your Resume

Now that you're equipped with tips for seeking your first job, let's get that position—let's craft a resume that will catch the eye of potential employers. A resume is your gateway to getting seen. It's your opportunity to make a strong impression and show potential employers that you're the right fit for the job. After all, employers receive numerous applications, and a well-crafted resume can help you stand out from the crowd and land that interview.

Your resume will be short and sweet, considering you're new to the working world and won't have much work experience to list. But that's perfectly okay. The length of your resume isn't the primary focus here. What truly matters is the message it leaves employers. Remember, everyone's out for the same thing. By submitting a resume, you set yourself apart from the competition. Don't skip the resume because you think there isn't much to spotlight. You know who else thinks that? The other kid you're competing with. So, create one.

Whether you use a template or create one from scratch, approach it with the same seriousness as a final essay. Be meticulous in how you organize and present information, and be sure to triple-check your resume for proper grammar and punctuation. This document reflects you and creates the first and last impression on potential employers, so make it count. Polish it to its final draft, displaying your best self on paper. While templates provide an easy jumpstart, they're available to anyone, so take the time to develop a personalized version. And don't forget to regularly update your resume to reflect new experiences and achievements you bring to the table.

Now, fire up your computer and compose a well-structured and professional-looking resume, making sure to include the following elements:

- Header: Display your first and last name, mailing address, phone number, and email.

- Objective Statement: Include a concise yet impactful objective statement, such as "Seeking a part-time position that allows me to apply my friendly demeanor to provide excellent customer service."

- Interests and Skills: List your interests and skills. When listing skills, include not only technical or tangible skills but soft skills like critical thinking and problem-solving, which are equally, if not more, important.

- Experience: List any knowledge and expertise obtained from previous work, school events, or community projects. For each entry, include the date and a brief description of tasks and responsibilities. Organize the list chronologically for clarity and neatness.

The overall presentation of your resume should reflect your thoughtfulness and attention to detail. Once finished, make a few copies and keep them readily available when it comes time to complete a job application. When visiting a job site to inquire about open positions or request an application, remember to bring along a copy of your resume—encased in a folder—so it remains nice and crisp.

Submitting your resume with an application is an excellent practice. It demonstrates your professionalism and preparedness, and many hiring managers appreciate it. Having your resume readily available on the spot solidifies your first impression, further increasing your chances of being noticed and considered for the job.

To ramp up your resume, consider customizing it to match the job you're applying for; it highlights your sincere interest in the position and emphasizes that you're not simply submitting generic applications to various employers. Pay attention to keywords and requirements in the job description and tailor your resume to those specifics.

Additionally, based on the position and expected qualifications, you can top off your resume with a cover letter. A cover letter adds a personal touch and allows you to express your enthusiasm for the job and gratitude for being considered. It's also the place where you can request an interview. Remember, you want to take the extra steps to place yourself at the forefront of the selection to enhance your chances of landing the job. It's the frosting on the cake—from mmm to ohhh.

Applying for the Job

You've got your resume perfected; now it's time to take the next step and inquire about job opportunities. When you're preparing to apply for a job, dress for success. It doesn't mean you must wear a suit and tie, but aim to look presentable and well-groomed. Even if all you have are jeans in your closet, pair them with something that gives you a clean and put-together appearance, such as a white collared button-up shirt— and tuck it in. After investing time and effort into your resume, now is not the time to get sloppy.

Your appearance should match the professionalism of your resume. *Check your nails, check your teeth, check your face, and check your hair.* Employers may not even give your qualifications a chance if your appearance puts them off. When making a positive first impression in the job market, appearance matters, as initial judgments are often based on looks. It's also worth checking your scent—just keeping it real!

Okay, your resume stands out. Your appearance also stands out. Now, let's get your job application to stand out—the final stage before that interview phone call.

Here are a few key points to keep in mind when filling out an application:

- Neatness: Complete the application in pen, neatly with your best handwriting.

- Thoroughness: Answer every question. If you can't provide an answer, write N/A (not applicable) to show that you've read through the questions and haven't skipped over them.

- Emphasis: Showcase your positive attributes, including punctuality, urgency, leadership, and attention to detail. Use language that conveys your eagerness and genuine desire for the job.

- Capability: List any experience that points to your suitability for the position. Here's where your crisp resume comes in handy. You can write down "see attached resume" in this section, and you're all set.

Don't feel discouraged if you lack a resume or formal work experience. What's even more important to employers is not just the prior jobs you've held but the qualities that define you as a person. So, think of experiences demonstrating responsibility, reliability, dedication, and other positive traits that make you a valuable candidate. These qualities will set you apart and make you a strong contender for the job. Whatever you do, avoid leaving the experience section blank.

What to Expect

You'll typically work around 15 to 20 hours a week, varying depending on your preferences and availability. Part-time jobs are designed to be flexible and fit into your schedule without interfering with school commitments. As such, there is a limit to the number of hours you can work on school days. Your school should provide you with this information and approve your work permit. You must submit the permit to your employer to ensure they comply with the authorized number of working hours as well as other guidelines.

As a part-time employee, you'll need to track your work hours by clocking in and out, which can be done through a physical timecard or an electronic system provided by your employer. Your pay is based on the total number of hours you've worked at your hourly rate, often the minimum wage determined by your state. Typically, you'll get paid every two weeks, and you can collect your paycheck during your next shift or on the designated payday. If you've signed up for direct deposit, your earnings will be electronically sent to your bank account—it's like having a personal money chute.

If you haven't thought about working while attending high school, it's worth considering. Employers who hire teenagers often recognize the need for flexibility and can create shift schedules that fit around your school commitments. Even if you can only dedicate a few hours each week to work part-time while in school, the experience provides a valuable opportunity to develop money skills such as expense tracking and saving *and* essential life skills such as time-management, communication, and problem-solving.

But there's more to it than that. The money you earn from your part-time job falls under the category of "earned income," and its role becomes particularly crucial in a central aspect of this book—investing. We'll navigate this exciting topic in the later chapters, and you'll better understand its significance and how it can impact your financial journey.

EXPLORING FREELANCING

Think of the skills you possess. Do you write well? Are you a math wizard? Can you fix computers or bikes? Are you good at graphic design? What about photography? Let's explore another way of earning "earned income" by utilizing your skills. Instead of the traditional part-time job where you work for an employer, consider freelancing, where you work for yourself. Freelancing is when you apply your skills and talents to complete specific jobs requested by individuals or businesses. You would take on a particular gig, perform the work as outlined, and receive payment once it's finished.

Flexibility and Autonomy

Freelancing offers a flexible way to earn money, and it can be an excellent option for you, as you already possess the skills required to perform the work. You can choose who you work for, what projects you take on, and your work hours as long as you meet the agreed-upon deadlines and deliver quality work (Downey, 2023). The bonus of freelancing is that it allows you to refine your skills, making the work more enjoyable and satisfying while improving your expertise. So, if you have multiple skills to offer and prefer an independent work style with flexibility in how and when you work, freelancing may be a good choice.

Searching for Gigs

You can find freelance gigs online or in your local community. However, before diving in, conduct further research to get a comprehensive understanding and feel of this venture. Unlike the straightforward nature of applying for part-time jobs, freelancing demands more from you. You'll take on the responsibility of actively searching out gigs, marketing yourself, reaching out to potential clients, and managing projects from beginning to end, all of which require substantial effort and commitment. So, although freelancing has its perks of flexibility and autonomy, the considerable amount of time and work involved in finding and managing gigs can be a little bit of a downer—something to think about. But hey, if you've got the talent people actively seek and know how to roll the dice—downer shnowner.

Maintaining Gig Records

As a freelancer, you're your boss, which means you'll need to manage your gig money (Downey, 2023). You must track your income and expenses and maintain thorough records. As cumbersome as it may seem, it's a must. Detailed descriptions of completed projects, including dates, clients, earnings, and expenses, will help you stay organized for tax filing time—a big headache in and of itself already. Unlike part-time jobs, where employers maintain your earnings records and pay taxes on your behalf, you're on your own as a freelancer; you'll need to pay those taxes yourself—it's your contribution to the well-being of this great nation.

Taxes can be quite intricate and often less exciting than personal finance. Fortunately, you don't need to understand the ins and outs of taxes; you just need to pay them when they're due, and you're good to go. A simple way to ensure you meet your tax obligations is to set aside at least 15% of your earnings into a dedicated "sinking fund" (Walrack, 2023), which we'll discuss ahead. Doing so, you'll be prepared to cover any owed amounts when it's time to file taxes.

Whether working a part-time job or freelancing, it's essential to approach making money responsibly. If you work for an employer, show up on time and take pride in your duties. If you've accepted a gig, follow through on your promises to clients. Take this opportunity to develop skills beyond making money, such as teamwork, communication, ownership, leadership, and grit. These skills aren't just valuable for your current role; they will serve you well throughout your life. So remember, when it comes to making money, it's not just about the earnings but the skills and character you develop and retain along the way—a proud parent moment. *Soak it all in, embrace the growth, and let this be your time to shine.*

FILLING OUT NEW-HIRE EMPLOYMENT FORMS

Before earning, there's a bit of paperwork involved. If you've accepted a part-time job, your employer will require you to complete several new-hire employment forms as part of the standard hiring process. We'll go through them here. Don't worry; we'll tackle this section just like we did with the bank statement—swiftly, breezing through the oh-so-boring class assignment. Now, if you're freelancing, these new-hire forms won't apply to you because, again, you're your boss. As such, your paperwork takes on an individualized approach. You'll create self-made forms outlining the project details, including client information, tasks, deadlines, and payment terms.

Here are some new-hire employment forms to take note of:

- W-4 Form: The W-4, or Employee's Withholding Certificate, informs your employer how much to withhold from your gross pay and then forward to the government for federal income tax. Accurately completing the form ensures that the correct amount of tax gets withheld from your paychecks throughout the year.

- I-9 Form: The I-9, or Employment Eligibility Verification, confirms your identity and work eligibility in the United States. It's a requirement for both you and your employer.

- State Tax Withholding Form: This form is similar to the W-4 but for state tax. Each state has its specific form.

- Direct Deposit Form: This form instructs your employer to electronically deposit your earnings into your bank account instead of issuing you a paper check. You'll still receive a detailed pay stub for your records.

- Emergency Contact Form: This form contains pertinent information about whom to contact in case of a workplace accident.

- Internal Company Forms: Companies have their own unique set of rules and policies, and these forms serve as a guide for you to behave accordingly. By following the specific rules and policies outlined in these forms, your actions will remain aligned with company culture. In other words, do what you were hired to do and don't engage in any activities you're not supposed to—or you may risk getting fired.

Practical Exercise: Practice Filling Out the W-4 and I-9
Download copies of the W-4 and I-9 and fill them out as practice. You'll feel more confident handling the documents in the Human Resources (HR) office. HR does all the hiring and firing—and everything that happens in between, including issuing paychecks. Get to know them.

DECODING YOUR PAYCHECK

Payday! The moment you've been waiting for—where your hard work pays off, and the paycheck finally lands in your hands. Whether it's hustling after school, tackling those duties like a champ, or just rocking a bright smile on the job, it's all worth it. You rip off the money part and toss the other part away. But hold on! That other part—your pay stub—is essential for understanding the fruits of your labor. So, dig it out, and let's go for another quick run-through.

A pay stub shows a breakdown of your earnings and deductions for a specific pay period, including taxes and benefits.

It provides a snapshot of where your hard-earned money is allocated. The format and exact details may vary depending on your employer and state.

Below are the typical components on your pay stub decoded:

- Regular Hours: The number of hours you work.

- Overtime Hours: The number of hours you work beyond regular hours.

- Standard Pay Rate: Your pay rate for regular hours.

- Overtime Pay Rate: Your pay rate for overtime hours.

- Gross Pay: The amount you earn before deductions are considered.

- Net Pay: The amount you take home after deductions are considered.

- Vacation and Sick: The number of paid leave days you have available for use.

- Bonus: A reward you receive for outstanding work performance.

- Federal, State, and Local Taxes: The amounts your employer withholds from your gross pay to fund government programs and services benefiting individuals and communities.

- Social Security and Medicare Taxes: The amounts your employer withholds from your gross pay to fund government programs supporting older individuals' living and medical expenses.

- Other Deductions: Various amounts subtracted from your gross pay for benefit plans you've enrolled in, such as retirement, health insurance, and life insurance.

That's essentially it—those are the main components of your pay stub. How quick was that? If you have any questions or need further clarification about the information on your pay stub, visit your Human Resources office, as they're the company experts in employment law.

The pay stub won't apply to you if you're a freelancer. As a self-employed individual, payments for completed gigs will be received in total, with no deductions and withholdings (Fishman, n.d.)— precisely why you should set aside at least 15% of your earnings for taxes, as previously explained. Setting it aside as you earn is a best practice.

Practical Exercise: Analyze Your Pay Stub
When you get paid, don't toss your pay stub. Use a calculator to break down each of its elements and understand their correlation. Identifying which items affect one another ensures you're being paid accurately.

EMBRACING A ROCK-SOLID WORK ETHIC

Juggling school and work goes beyond attending classes and punching timecards at the job. It's a well-rehearsed performance where you're mastering the art of time management and developing essential character traits and skills. You're building a strong reputation that can open countless doors in your future, and it's fueling a *rock-solid work ethic*.

Embrace this opportunity to grow and excel academically and professionally. Think about how the experience will positively impact your college applications, job interviews, and your career path. It's not just about making a few extra dollars—it's about leveling up in real life! Your early start, dedication, and hard work can lead to scholarships, promotions, and your ultimate dream job.

Being a student and employee at a young age is no small feat. It speaks volumes about your unwavering commitment. Despite enduring an entire day attending school and still having hours of homework ahead, you consistently find the energy and enthusiasm to put in those four hours at work—serving customers, tidying up aisles, handling carts, and cleaning up spills. Your journey is just beginning, and there's no doubt you'll continue to excel as you ascend the steps of life.

Keep up the fantastic work!

4

————✕————

Assigning Roles to Your Money

Think of money as a team of players, much like in a soccer match. You have defenders, midfielders, strikers, and goalkeepers. Each player has a specific role; when they work together strategically, they win games. Your money can work the same way. Instead of spending all your money foolishly, which is like sending all your players to attack without a game plan, you can assign unique roles to your money and create a financial strategy.

This chapter will discuss three critical roles for your money: implementing a zero-based budget to allocate every dollar you earn, building an emergency fund for peace of mind, and creating sinking funds for planned expenses. The role of investing, a significant player in your financial strategy, will be covered in a separate chapter, as it's a total game-changer on its own. Stay tuned for in-depth insights and practical guidance, where we unravel its mysteries and potential rewards, taking your financial game to the next level.

IMPLEMENTING A ZERO-BASED BUDGET: ROLE #1

A budget is a practical financial tool that helps you proactively manage your money. Its primary purpose is to ensure that your income covers your expenses. Some find the term "budget" dreadful, but it's a financial tool everyone needs. Just like you wouldn't go on a road trip without a GPS, you shouldn't navigate your financial life without a budget. Your money isn't wandering aimlessly in the world of money consumption but actively leads you to financial wins.

Enter the *zero-based budget*—a powerful extension of traditional budgeting that goes beyond covering expenses—it also takes into account short-term and long-term savings goals and debt repayments (Schwahn, 2022). The core idea is simple: *Every dollar you earn has a purpose, and every dollar should be allocated to a designated category before the month begins.* At the end of the month, your income minus your everyday spending, recurring expenses, savings goals, and debt repayments should equal, you guessed it, zero—this signals that each dollar has served its purpose as planned.

Despite its name, the "zero" in zero-based budgeting is not set in stone. You can define your zero point, the amount of money you'd like to keep as a buffer for minor unexpected expenses or simply for peace of mind. Depending on your objectives and comfort level, this buffer amount can be $50, $100, $200, or any other amount. If you prefer not to have this buffer, zero can be $0, but I recommend having a buffer. Let's say you set your buffer at $200. It's not a free pass to spend it down to $0; it's still your zero. Your $200 needs to sit there for the just-in-case's—like if you need to top off your gas tank due to extra driving for a busy month of activities.

While numerous budgeting apps can automate this process, starting with pen and paper can provide better understanding of your spending habits. If you're not currently working and still under your parents' support, budgeting may not feel immediately applicable. However, let me emphasize the critical role of budgeting in financial management—*it's the essence of effectively managing your money!*

Creating a zero-based budget is a straightforward process, and the idea is simple to grasp—your income minus your expenses, savings, and debts should equal zero. It's that easy. However, don't underestimate its simplicity. The impact lies in its implementation, but implementation begins with creation. So, when you start earning, remember to create a zero-based budget and leave no financial stone unturned.

Here's how to create a zero-based budget for your money:

Step One: Create a Zero-Based Budget Worksheet

1. Title a piece of paper, such as August Budget.

2. Identify your monthly income, which can come from a part-time job, freelance gigs, or allowances.

3. Determine how much to allocate toward savings goals.

4. Decide how much to allocate toward debt repayments.

5. Create a list of expense categories, such as gas, snacks, eating out, and entertainment, and allocate a reasonable amount for each type to establish your planned spending limits.

6. Define your zero point, your buffer.

7. Subtract your expenses, savings, and debts from your income; the result should equal to zero or your buffer. Adjust your allocations as necessary.

Step Two: Create Expense Tracking Worksheets

1. Create an Expense Tracking Worksheet for each of your expense categories.

2. Design each Expense Tracking Worksheet with four columns: Date, Merchant, Amount, and Running Total.

Step Three: Track Your Daily Expenses

1. Collect receipts as you spend throughout the day.

2. Transfer purchase details from your receipts to the Expense Tracking Worksheets.

3. Calculate and record the amounts for each category separately onto the Expense Tracking Worksheets for those receipts covering multiple categories. Consider categorizing items during checkout.

4. Maintain a running total as new purchases accumulate on the Expense Tracking Worksheets.

Step Four: Calculate and Record

1. Total your purchases from the Expense Tracking Worksheets at the end of the month.

2. Record these totals onto the Budget Worksheet you created in Step One.

Step Five: Review and Adjust

1. Review your spending against your planned limits.

2. Adjust your expense categories for next month if necessary; shift funds from overestimated to underestimated categories.

Step Six: Repeat the Steps for Next Month's Budget

As you budget monthly, remain proactive by regularly monitoring your progress and evaluating your spending midway through the month—this gives you time to adjust. If you find yourself nearing your spending limits or possibly exceeding your budget, ask yourself the following questions to help you determine the best course of action:

- Am I on track to stay within my budget?
- What are my big expenses so far, and can I reduce them?
- Are there unnecessary purchases I can avoid?
- Can I shift funds around to cover unexpected costs?

By creating a budget, you're not just allocating your money where it needs to go but also creating space for what you want. If you think of it this way—as a permission slip that allows you to spend responsibly—budgeting becomes less restricting. Spending on something you want doesn't make you feel as guilty when you've already allocated for your needs. You can have our cake (needs) and eat it too (wants)!

So, whether you're working toward a car purchase, building an emergency fund, investing in your future, or saving for an extended vacation, implementing a zero-based budget can pave the way to achieving these financial goals. As you witness its effectiveness, it no longer feels like a chore. Instead, you'll look forward to setting financial milestones with enthusiasm and determination.

For hands-on budgeting worksheets, grab a copy of my *Zero-Based Budgeting Guide* located after the Table of Contents. You'll find an easy yet practical approach to maximize every hard-earned dollar. Even if budgeting is currently not on your radar, grab it anyway—it gives you a helpful visual of the concept. The guide is a free bonus, so there's nothing to lose. Simply scan the QR Code or visit the URL shown on that page to claim your copy!

BUILDING AN EMERGENCY FUND: ROLE #2

Life is a whirlwind of surprises. Some surprises are great, like acing a test you thought was doomed or discovering bonus fries hidden at the bottom of the bag. However, some surprises aren't so great—like your car suddenly sputtering to a halt on the freeway. When situations like this happen, having access to immediate funds—your *emergency fund*—can provide instant stress relief and peace of mind.

An emergency fund serves as your financial safety net, a dedicated reserve to rescue yourself from those "Oh, no!" moments that catch you off guard. And let's be clear: This safety net isn't your credit card. While the plastic might swiftly get your car towed and ensure a safe ride home, it's not the hero in this story. Who will rescue you from the credit card chaos it can create? Your emergency fund, however, is your reliable superhero, a stash of cash waiting for the unforeseen. It's the financial fortress *you've* built (yes, you build it) to weather the storms without relying on credit cards, only to avoid dealing with their aftermath. Glitter makes everything better, but imagine cleaning the mess—what a pain.

So, before that unforeseen life event happens, let's build up your emergency fund:

1. Start With a Goal of $1,000: Why $1,000? It's a sensible starting point. It's sufficient to cover most minor emergencies but not so daunting that it feels unattainable.

2. Extend Your Budgeting Skills: Building an emergency fund is a natural extension of your budgeting skills. Include a dedicated line item in your budget for your emergency fund and decide on the amount you'll save. It's like a mini-budget within a budget.

3. Define a Savings Schedule: Determine whether you'll save your preplanned amount weekly, bi-weekly, or monthly, and mark these dates on your calendar.

4. Build It Up Fast: Your emergency fund isn't something you're saving up for in the distant future. It's for, well, emergencies, and those can strike at any time. Strive to grow it as rapidly as you can. Once it's built up, lock it down and label it "For Emergency Only."

5. Build It Up More: You're not fully independent yet, but it's never too early to start saving for when you're off on your own. The goal is to have three to six months of future living expenses saved up (Tarpley, 2023)—rough estimates will do. It may be a slow process, but keep this thought alive. No matter what, you'll need this super-charged safety net, so there's no harm in steadily accumulating your savings. Think: What will happen if you lose your job? With at least three months' worth of expenses covered, you'll have a cushion while searching for a new and improved position.

Once you've established this emergency fund, you've taken another big step toward financial responsibility and stability. It demonstrates your ability to plan, make intelligent choices, and take control of your money. Building the fund involved a ton of sacrifices. Now, *don't touch it unless you're facing an emergency*. If you must use it, replenish it as soon as possible.

In the story of the Three Little Pigs, the pigs quickly rebuilt their house with sticks after the Big Bad Wolf came and blew their straw house down. And later, with bricks, not knowing when the Big Bad Wolf would show its face again. Similarly, when life's unexpected huffs and puffs reach your front door, your solid emergency fund can withstand a few loose bricks. A few bricks knocked loose is much easier to rebuild than a complete collapse.

You can never rebuild this fund back up fast enough. Your emergency fund, once utilized, becomes a priority to rebuild, just like those wise little pigs, reinforcing their home with sticks and again later with bricks. So, like the diligent builder pig, each contribution to your emergency fund adds another layer of financial bricks, constructing a fortress that stands strong against the face of uncertainty.

Keep It Boring

Your emergency fund has one sole purpose: to lie dormant in your savings account, collecting digital dust and doing nothing—not even investing! It's the dullest money you'll ever have. Trust me, you don't want it to be exciting. You want peace of mind knowing that you can outsmart the Big Bad Wolf without sinking into debt or being burdened by stress. In personal finance, *a boring emergency fund gets the job done.*

As tempting as investing your emergency fund money may be, resist the urge. We'll get into investing soon, but it's crucial to emphasize here that *the money you anticipate needing within five years should not be put into the stock market,* a virtual place where people buy and sell investments (Brock, 2023). The stock market's value constantly fluctuates, and when it's down, there may not be enough time to recover investment losses if you need your funds for emergencies or short-term goals. You don't want your $10,000 emergency fund valued at $7,000 when you need the entire $10,000. So, firmly stick to the notion that your emergency fund is not an investment fund—it must be readily available with full access whenever, wherever. It needs to be ready for the Big Bad Wolf.

Begin Your Fund—Now

The perfect time to start building an emergency fund is when life's pretty quiet—like now, while you're still under your parents' roof. With their support meeting your basic needs, you have the opportunity to work, save, and repeat the process. While building up to six months on minimum wage may seem like a far reach, see it as an end goal rather than an overnight achievement; it can help you see the point in every dollar set aside. Once you venture out on your own, having already built up this safety net allows you to forge along, freeing you up to focus on maximizing your money in other areas of your life. Start building it now and think of it as your quiet guardian, ready to lift you when life throws curveballs.

CREATING SINKING FUNDS: ROLE #3

You've got dreams—maybe it's buying your first car *and* having enough money to start a new hobby. The key to achieving both is through the use of sinking funds. While your emergency fund is reserved for the unexpected, sinking funds serve a different purpose—they're for the *expected*. These funds offer a strategic approach to saving for future goals or handling repeat, non-monthly expenses. Creating sinking funds is straightforward; you can easily set them up through your bank, assigning each one an appropriate name, such as Car Sinking Fund and Hobby Sinking Fund.

This concept of sinking funds was introduced earlier when discussing freelancing—do you recall the suggestion to set aside 15% of earnings into a dedicated sinking fund for taxes? Since taxes are a repeat non-monthly expected expense, creating a sinking fund for them makes sense.

Imagine sinking funds as labeled jars for your money, each representing a separate savings account for various goals or non-monthly expenses. Picture one jar dedicated to your car, a second jar for your hobby, and a third for your annual academic subscription. Consistently building up these sinking funds throughout the year is like filling up each jar until you can redeem them for your goals. This physical separation eliminates any guesswork, showing precisely how much is set aside for each goal. And you don't feel like you're sacrificing one goal for the other. When you cash in the first jar, you'll free up dollars to fill the remaining jars even faster.

What's even better is that sinking funds make your goals feel achievable by breaking them into manageable monthly increments. Saving for a car feels less discouraging when you witness your Car Sinking Fund growing steadily each month.

This practical approach instills confidence that your goals are within reach and that future expenses will be covered. So, whether it's saving up for a new set of wheels or preparing for a new hobby, sinking funds turns your dreams into tangible accomplishments.

Practical Exercise: Create a Sinking Fund

Think of something you want to save for and create a sinking fund through your bank. Figure out how much the item will cost, divide it by the number of months until you want to buy it, and that's how much you'll save each month. Then, track your progress and celebrate as you get closer to your goal.

5

---∞---

Putting Your Money to Work

Investing: your hard-earned money's fourth and most impactful role. Investing isn't a far-off concept meant only for the super-rich. In fact, if you want to be super rich, then investing *is* for you. It opens the door to growing your riches beyond what traditional savings can achieve.

Schools aren't handing out lesson plans about how to grow your money tree, and your parents, juggling everything life throws at them, want you to learn this stuff ASAP. So, let's shed some light on the subject. It's time you give your money the ultimate job, the kind where it earns its keep and isn't lazing around in your bank account—it's hustling for you. Remember that $250,000 government-insured idle money? Most of that must be put to work.

It's natural to want to treat yourself to nice things. Whether it's the latest shoulder bag, new clothes, or a nice set of Apple EarPods, temptations are all around. Sure, that's fun for like a minute. But let's bring it up several notches. Let's invest your money! Think of your paychecks not just as a ticket to immediate stuff but as a ticket to your future freedom. A portion of it is all you need. You're going to love it. So put on your party hat and grab some noise makers because you're about to make your money move!

How Does Investing Even Work?

Investing isn't rocket science, I promise. When you invest, you're essentially lending your money to a company or a government, and they repay you with interest (free money). Alternatively, you're buying a tiny slice of a company, and if the company does well, so do you (again, free money). The idea is, over time, that money grows exponentially thanks to *compound interest*. We'll immerse in this "magic trick" phenomenon, but for now, say it with me: *"compound interest."*

You're young, and time is your greatest asset. The remarkable thing about compound interest is that it doesn't ask for a lot of your money. It just asks for your time. The more time you give it, the more money it gives you. As a teen, you've got lots of time; if you give it to compound interest, it will reward you beyond your imagination. Do you know how a garden weed can flourish from nothing? Kind of like that.

But Isn't Investing Risky?

Okay, let's address the elephant in the room. You've probably heard people say investing is risky. And yes, like some things in life, it has its risks. But listen up: Not investing is risky, too. Imagine tucking all your money under your bed. Sure, it's safe, but it's not growing. Over time, that money loses value due to inflation—basically, the rising cost of stuff. I mean, a box of Lucky Charms is about $6 now!

Various investments carry different levels of risk and potential for reward. The key is to *minimize risk* while *maximizing reward.* How do you balance this? By acquiring knowledge and sticking to sound, time-tested principles. As I mentioned at the outset of this book, I won't be guiding you on a journey to quick wealth. *It's the pursuit of rapid riches that carries the most risk.* Investing patiently and steadily is low-risk and it's what yields maximum rewards.

After completing this book, you'll better understand the level of "risk" involved and shift your focus from a risk mentality to a reward mentality. You'll realize that any perceived risk is minimal compared to the potential long-term rewards. We're not aiming for risky home runs. Instead, we're eagle-eye focused on consistently hitting those singles and doubles.

Besides, you *can* afford to take these small risks at your age because you have plenty of time to ride out the so-called "ups and downs" of the stock market. When the market is up, your investments are gaining value; when the market is down, your investments are losing value. It's the inherent nature of the stock market to fluctuate. Take comfort in the fact that, over the long term, these temporary dips appear as potholes compared to the overall potential growth trajectory. So, don't be discouraged by the risks; they are a natural part of the investment journey.

Where Do I Start?

You're going to start with a Roth IRA. You'll learn about this in Chapters 7 and 8. If you're not yet 18, you'll need a parent or legal guardian to assist you in opening an investment account. So, this may be the perfect time to preview this idea with them. *Break the cycle.* Be the one in your family to say, "Hey, we should be talking about this stuff." I don't know any parent who won't listen to their kids about money skills.

What if I Mess Up?

That's okay! Isn't that how we all learn, through making initial mistakes first? But don't worry; I'll help you through this. There is one mess-up you should avoid, however—and that is *not* investing at all. Besides, we're steering clear of a high-risk, high-reward strategy in this investing game. Instead, we're going for a low-risk, high-diversification, high-reward strategy. It may be a bit of a tongue-twister, but it perfectly sums up our philosophy to investing.

Let me explain. In investing, there's something referred to as *diversification*, a key factor in reducing risk (Royal, 2023). It involves spreading your money across different investments to reduce financial risk and still make money (Royal, 2023). We'll use this strategy to knock the ball out of the park. You'll hear investors say, "Don't put all your eggs in one basket," as a reference to diversification. So, don't worry about the possibility of messing up—because we'll be scattering our eggs all around.

What Should I Invest In?

Sometimes, in life, the more options you have, the more difficult it is to make a decision. For me, it's standing in front of the donut counter, trying to decide between custard, twist, crumb, powder, buttermilk, sprinkle, and sugar. And do you know what I end up with? Just a plain ol' glazed—simple and best, anyway.

The same holds for investing. You have options like stocks, bonds, money market funds, index funds, exchange-traded funds, real estate, and commodities. Having choices is better than having none, but an overwhelming number tends to leave people feeling paralyzed, weighed down, hesitant to learn, and fearful of taking action.

My friend, I won't let you become one of these people—because we're sticking to "plain ol' glazed," a.k.a. *index funds*.

Index funds are like your giant teddy bear, still hiding somewhere in your closet. Like Big Teddy, your index fund will be there for you at the beginning of your investment journey and will continue to be there even when you're too busy to give it attention. And just like Big Teddy, the longer you hang on to your index fund, the more you'll grow to appreciate what it has done for you. *Index funds are the heart and soul of your investments*, and you'll discover all of their wonders in Chapter 10. I can't wait for you to get there.

Do I Need a Financial Advisor?

Nah. The techniques in this book can empower you to make informed decisions without needing professional help. Remember, we're aiming to keep investing simple. Plus, there's a wealth of information available online—and don't underestimate the value of an excellent financial literacy book for teens (wink). Armed with the proper knowledge, you can become a wise young investor beyond your years. Financial advisors come into play if, for whatever reason, your finances get too complicated to handle on your own. But why do that?

As a teen, simplicity in investing is key. The last thing you need, besides doing homework, studying for tests, and clocking in work hours, is adding complexity to your money and feeling the need to hire a pro. The goal is to set you up for financial success without making things harder than they need to be. Feeling overwhelmed can be a real deal-breaker.

HARNESSING COMPOUND INTEREST AND TIME

You know what's insane? We've been taught Pythagoras's theorem and how cells divide, but no one ever sat us down to talk about compound interest and how it could transform our financial lives. Yep, that's right—the subject notably absent from your school curriculum is one of the most potent forces in the financial universe. Just because you're a teen doesn't mean you can't grasp it. So why isn't it taught? Who knows. It's now time to take control of your financial education and equip yourself with the knowledge and tools to navigate the world of money. *You got this*. Here goes.

Compound Interest: The What

Compound interest is the process of earning interest on the initial amount of money you invest (the principal) and *all* the interest you earned from previous periods (Bennett, 2023). Compounding grows money at a mind-blowing accelerated rate and is a powerful force in building wealth. However, compounding works in both directions; it can also deplete your money at a mind-blowing accelerated rate—think credit cards. This financial phenomenon doesn't discriminate; *it rewards those who invest wisely and punishes those who accumulate debt without a clear plan*. It's a force to be reckoned with, and you'll learn to steer compound interest in the right direction and harness it to your advantage. And when you get it, it'll become one of your favorite things.

81

Compound Interest: The Snowball Effect

Imagine you're rolling a snowball down a hill. At first, it's tiny. As it moves and gathers more snow, it grows larger. That's how compound interest works—your money earns a little, and then that earned money earns even more, and the cycle continues. Before you know it, that tiny snowball you started with has turned into a mammoth-sized ball of wealth.

Compound Interest: The Money Pet

Have you ever thought about how money could be like a pet? Of course not. But let's go with it. Imagine having a little money pet that makes baby money pets. Yeah, it's weird. You feed it by investing, and then it grows. The baby money pets also grow up and start having their babies. Over time, you've got a whole money pet zoo multiplying right under your nose. That's compound interest for you—turning your small money pet into a large family of multiplying investments.

Compound Interest: The Killer Drum Solo

One more analogy to drive the point home: Compound interest is like that killer drum solo in the middle of your favorite band's epic song—except it keeps building on itself, and the crescendo never stops. It's a financial beat that keeps going and growing, creating a rhythm of wealth with every passing note. Your investments are the instruments, and compound interest is the conductor that leads them to an ever-expanding crescendo. What a visual.

Okay, forget those analogies. Take it from the genius Albert Einstein: *"Compound interest is the eighth wonder of the world. He who understands it, earns it; he who doesn't, pays it"* (Quotes on Finance, n.d.). These words from one of the greatest minds in history highlight the profound impact of compound interest on your financial life. Understanding and harnessing the power of compound interest can be the key to your financial success. It's not just a clever concept; it's a force that can either work for you or against you. And by learning about it, you're taking a huge step to ensure it works in your favor.

Seize the Advantage of Time

Why should you prioritize harnessing the power of compound interest when there's so much else to do and think about? Albert Einstein eloquently emphasized the first part of the answer. Here's the second part: You have abundant time on your side. As you venture into your first job, whether flipping burgers or coding, you're set to reap the rewards for your hard work. The decisions you make with your money at that pivotal juncture can either make or break your financial journey. *Invest some: level up. Spend it all: game over.*

So, while you have finals to study for, a long essay to write, a group project to finish, and friends to meet, compound interest doesn't demand your active time and energy. You simply need to grasp its worth, complete this book, and flip the *on* switch. Then, you won't need to "stress" about it. You can still study for your finals, write your essay, finish your group project, meet up with your friends, and do everything else you put in your schedule while leveling up.

There's a tendency to think that you have all the time in the world, but that's a bit of a mirage. You blink, and suddenly, you're graduating, moving out, and beginning your career. Time has this sneaky habit of accelerating when you least expect it, which is precisely why you need to harness the precious time you've got now.

Life comes at you fast, but your money can grow even faster if you grab hold of this powerful force and direct its energy. Investing even $10 a month can earn you five figures over time (Investor.gov, n.d.). Yes, it's *that* powerful. Can you imagine what you can achieve by consistently investing a little more? I'm not talking about just money. I'm talking about the freedom to choose *what's next*. If you're tired of working, what's next is quitting (because you can). If you're unhappy with your current location, what's next is to relocate (because you can). If you've never traveled to other countries, what's next is planning your dream destination (because you can). The power to mold your future is within your reach. And it starts with $10. Believe it.

Compound interest is magical on its own, but when you add the component of time, you'll be skyrocketing to the moon and back. The more time you feed into compound interest, the bigger your snowball becomes, the faster your money pet zoo multiplies, and the louder the drum solo grows. Then, you'll totally get what Albert Einstein is saying.

"Okay, but I'm just a teen, and investing seems like such a hard concept."

I understand that. But you've mastered social media algorithms and the intricacies of TikTok dances (or at least, you know what I'm getting at). Believe it or not, you already possess the skillset to understand this fundamental financial principle of compound interest and time. All that remains is the discipline to start early, the patience to grow your money, and the knowledge you'll gain from this book.

Your choices today will give you a head start or put you in catch-up mode for years. *You don't have to learn money lessons the hard way.* Leverage this concept of compound interest and time to pull ahead of the curve, let your money start working for you, and prove you can do it.

The Marathon Mentality

You may see stories about people becoming millionaires by investing in the "next big thing." Those stories are the exceptions, not the norms. Building wealth through investments is an intentional, steady journey, not a shortcut to quick riches.

Allowing FOMO (Fear of Missing Out) or YOLO (You Only Live Once) to drive your investment decisions can lead to rapid gains and losses, resulting in unnecessary financial setbacks, demotivation, and doubts about the effectiveness of investing. Please steer clear of this mindset. Embrace a "slow and steady wins the race" approach and keep your wealth-building clean, smart, and anchored in solid strategies. Imagine that you're entering a marathon, not sprinting from the starting line.

Practical Exercise: Play With a Compound Interest Calculator
Compound interest calculators are your secret window into discovering your money's potential. Visit Investor.gov and locate the compound interest calculator. Plug in numbers to get a sneak peek into your financial future. See how much a certain sum of money would grow over 5, 10, 20, or even 40 years. It can be an instant motivator, inspiring you to make smarter financial decisions. *Caution: It can be addictive.*

6

———— ✕ ————

Cultivating Wealth

Your school teaches you about isosceles triangles and iambic pentameters but skips the low-down on making your money work for you. What gives? You learn algebra, but what about how to grow your savings? Silence. Zip. Nada. (Sorry to mention this gap in the school system again. Can you tell I wish I had learned this at your age?)

My friend, you want to be more than a cog in the machine. This chapter and the next few are your ticket out of that dreary cycle and into the wonders of wealth building, where you become the engineer of your financial success, not just another gear. It's time to break free from the limitations of the traditional education system and start from scratch. We'll design a reinforced, sturdy foundation for your bright future.

Building wealth isn't just about stacking Benjamins until you can't see over them, although that visual is entertaining. It's about understanding the value of money, making informed decisions, and putting those dollars to work for you. It's not just saving money. It's investing and creating passive income streams. Your unallocated money should never sit idle. It should be actively working for you, running laps, breaking a sweat, and training for the Money Olympics. Get it?

Do you ever think about your future? Scratch that—you definitely think about your future. Whether it's that sneaker drop you're saving for or the car you plan to buy when you get your driver's license, we all have things we're looking forward to. How cool would it be if you didn't have to dwell too hard before making those purchases or seizing the opportunity of a lifetime? *Your future doesn't have to remain a thought.*

"I get what you're saying and I'm on board with the idea. But why should I bother with it now? I'm young and have plenty of time to think about it later. I'm dealing with other priorities that already cause stress."

Let me share three compelling reasons to get you to bother:

First, yes, you've got plenty of time. But remember, time is a valuable resource that you can't renew. The sooner you begin building wealth, the more time you have for your money to work its magic and the less heavy lifting you'll have to do later. Does the term "compound interest" ring a bell?

Second, you don't want to fall into the dreaded paycheck-to-paycheck cycle. Many adults, unfortunately, find themselves trapped in a stressful life because they didn't learn these financial principles when they were your age. Being stuck in a never-ending loop of worrying about making ends meet is not where you want to find yourself, and I don't want you to experience that struggle.

Even worse, the absence of a proper financial foundation can lead you to chase one quick fix after another, getting caught in a sticky web of easy-to-get credit cards or high-interest loans. You think you're solving a problem, but really, you're just digging a deeper hole. Building wealth now ensures you won't fall into that hole. It'll provide you with a security blanket for the uncertainties life will inevitably toss your way.

Third, how about freedom? Yes, building wealth gives you freedom. It allows you to travel, learn new skills, and start exciting ventures without hesitation. So, while you're young, you have this unique opportunity to secure your financial future—and this unique opportunity, *once gone, it's gone.*

Money holds power, the power to define your choices and determine your quality of life. Take a moment right now to internalize that statement. Do these words resonate with you, even just a little? I hope so because this idea needs to sink deep, inspiring you to want to seize control of your financial destiny, build wealth now, and live freely later.

CHOOSING ASSETS OVER LIABILITIES

Investing is like a game of rock-paper-scissors, where assets constantly beat liabilities every time. This simple yet potent principle is the bedrock of wealth-building, and it's always a wise move to direct your money toward assets.

Assets are the major players that put money in your pocket—they're the positives in your net worth equation. They come in various forms, including real estate, such as a house or a piece of land; precious metals, like gold or silver; and the money you've saved or invested. Assets *appreciate*, meaning they increase in value or generate income over time, *inflating your net worth.*

On the flip side, liabilities are the formidable opponents that take money out of your pocket—they're the negatives. High-end smartphones purchased on a payment plan, weekends filled with extravagant shopping with friends, and burdensome car loans are all liabilities. Liabilities *depreciate*, meaning they decrease in value over time, *deflating your net worth.*

Think of your net worth as your financial IQ score, where a higher score is better. To calculate your net worth, subtract your total liabilities from your assets—or your negatives from your positives. For instance, imagine owning a house valued at $500,000, but you also owe $30,000 on your car loan, $20,000 on your student loan, and $1,000 on your credit card. Your net worth stands at $449,000, which highlights a crucial point: The more you owe, the less you have, even though the value of what you own is $500,000.

Understanding this equation—assets minus liabilities—is the core of managing and building wealth. As you move up life's ladder, you'll be forced to distinguish between assets and liabilities—and that requires discipline; the math around it is easy. Financial wisdom lies in making decisions where the math adds up right. The takeaway? Carefully work through each problem and choose wisely.

The cardinal rule of building wealth is clear as daylight: *Increase your assets and keep your liabilities in check.* It's as simple as that. By diligently following this principle, you'll stay on a steady course toward wealth accumulation.

However, executing this principle can only be "as simple as that" if you've laid the groundwork for a rock-solid financial mindset. Otherwise, it can be even more challenging than it naturally is. Getting good with money is a gradual process, which is why it's necessary to start early. Any mistakes you make early on are minor compared to the priceless lessons you'll gain. Consequently, you'll establish an unbreakable financial foundation where assets reign over liabilities.

GENERATING PASSIVE INCOME STREAMS

Have you ever heard of the saying "making money while you sleep?" It's a real thing. This concept is about passive income, which requires little effort to maintain, making it intriguing to many (Brock, 2023). Yet, starting a passive income stream may demand an initial investment of time or money and could involve a steep learning curve. But once set up successfully and flowing smoothly, passive income can provide a continuous source of added income, offering an effortless way to build wealth (Brock, 2023).

There are numerous ways to generate passive income, including YouTube content creation, stock photo sales, and app development. You can have multiple streams working for you if you're able. If it interests you, explore this concept on your own—countless ideas exist. In this book, you'll discover one of the most effortless passive income streams to build and maintain (hint: Chapter 8). Plus, it doesn't demand much time or investment for great results, and the learning curve isn't steep if you follow the strategy.

The concept of passive income is undeniably exciting. I mean, who wouldn't want to make money while hitting snooze? But understand that it's not something you rush into. Instead, it's something to be nurtured on the side while you're working on the main event: *your education and career.* Your education and career are *needs*, and passive income streams are *wants*. Remember the discussion about needs vs. wants?

LEVERAGING TIME

Why wait until you're 30 or 40 to start piling up the bucks? Let me share an example that illustrates why you shouldn't wait. It's eye-opening, awe-inspiring, and down-right empowering. So, brace yourself for this revealing example that will reshape your perspective on the urgency of starting now.

You: At age 20, you begin investing $100 monthly into an S&P 500 Index Fund (discussed later) with a historical annual average return of about 10% (Maverick, 2023). By age 65, your investment would reach $869,974.85, of which $54,000 came from your own money (Investor.gov., n.d.).

Bestie: Your friend, Bestie, doesn't start investing until age 40 and invests $500 monthly. Assuming all other factors remain equal, Bestie's investment would reach $595,499.71, of which $150,500 came from Bestie's own money (Investor.gov, n.d.).

Let's analyze it. Each month, you invested only one-fifth of what Bestie did ($100 vs. $500). In the end, you stashed away only about one-third of Bestie's total ($54,000 vs. $150,500). And yet—brace yourself—astoundingly, your final sum is approximately 46% more than Bestie's! *Mind-blowing!*

If this isn't magic, then I don't know what is. My friend, take this moment to reflect. Can you see why it's vital to leverage time to build wealth now? Look at those numbers again. Do you think you could invest $100 a month? How about $50? Or just $10? I believe you can. *There's no such thing as investing too little.* If you think $10 is too little to bother, think again. Investing $10 monthly for 45 years could reward you with— get ready—$86,977.49 (Investor.gov, n.d.).

"It took 45 years? Of course, my money would grow by that much. I don't see anything special here."

Fasten your seat belt: *Only* $5,410 came from your pocket! The remarkable growth in your investment is due to compounding. Remember the snowball effect? The money pet? The drum solo? And yes, the eighth wonder of the world?

Do you *see* the magic now? I bet this makes you want to tell Bestie. Who wouldn't like to share the secret to turning $10 into almost $90,000 with their best friend? Best friends share good things—and this is a really, really good thing.

THINKING LONG-TERM

Where do you see yourself in 40 years? That's a tricky question to answer. You're a teen, and a year seems like a century. I bet you're more focused on planning your next long weekend with Bestie than wondering about the distant future, and that's fine—it's all part of being a teen. But I need you to take a few seconds to listen to the voice of Future Self:

"When you can no longer rely on others or your income for financial support, the only person responsible for taking care of you—is you. Wouldn't you want to reach a point where you can stop working and enjoy the fruits of your labor? Being broke in retirement is not an option. Okay? It's easier to start building wealth now than it is to find it in retirement."

Now, that future may seem forever away, but when you prioritize building wealth, you're ensuring Future Self is prepared for life's bumps and bruises—Future Self is counting on you to invest now for retirement. Don't worry; you can still make room for those fun weekends with Bestie. Building wealth doesn't mean sacrificing your youth; it means setting yourself up for an incredible future full of $10 opportunities.

7

---- ∞ ----

Securing Your Future

Retirement marks the phase when you decide to leave the workforce for good. But here's the burning question: Who will pay for your day-to-day expenses and much-deserved vacations when that time rolls around? You guessed it—you! The government pitches in a little, and I emphasize a little. It'll barely cover your basic living costs, let alone those dream getaways. The weight of responsibility lies squarely on your shoulders, and you'll feel it getting heavier and heavier the longer you delay planning for your exit.

I sense that you're beginning to paint a picture of your future. It may be somewhat blurry, but it's one you may not have had when you started this book. Like a sixth sense, it's there but not quite there. You now perceive money as an extension of yourself, woven into your thoughts, actions, and character. You're embracing your newfound knowledge but still struggling to accept that you must worry about retirement now. The spark is ignited, but it has yet to evolve.

"I hear you, but retirement seems lightyears away, and I honestly don't think I need to care about old people's stuff right now. I mean, how many teenagers are thinking about it?"

It's completely understandable how this thought may linger, but what if I present it to you this way: "That person could be you sooner than you think. The old you will either thank you or curse you for your choices today." Early retirement planning is a serious matter, and that's why we're discussing it even at your age—to secure your future.

I'm sure you and your friends discuss plans after graduation, whether attending a local community college, a four-year university, a trade school, or joining the military. These discussions are natural because they revolve around what happens immediately after high school. However, it's interesting that while we're conditioned to care so much about our post-high school plans, nobody conditions us to care about our post-career plans—retirement.

Retirement isn't something high schoolers typically discuss, let alone fully comprehend, because it would be "weird." It doesn't occupy your thoughts like post-high school plans do. Nevertheless, now is the time you should start caring about it because before you know it, your career will end—just like high school will. You wouldn't want to be in a scramble, figuring out how to live the rest of your life without a regular paycheck while the bills keep coming.

What's that thing called again? That magical stuff that makes your money grow exponentially over time? Yes, you're right on the money. With the magic of compound interest churning by your side, you'll be taking vacation after vacation long before you can say, "I'm retiring." All this to say: Retirement is *not* light years away, and you *must* care about "old people's stuff" *right now*—at least the stuff of 401(k)s and IRAs.

401(k)s and IRAs aren't your typical run-of-the-mill savings accounts. They're your powerful allies in preparing you for the retirement phase of life. What makes them truly remarkable? First, they give you access to the stock market to grow your wealth; second, they allow your money to grow without being nibbled by taxes—*your money grows tax-free.*

When you earn money, taxes take a share of your income—it's a fact of life. But it doesn't stop there. Taxes also claim a portion of what your money makes. So, if you stash your cash in your bank's savings account and earn a small interest, taxes take a small bite. If you up your game and put your money into investments through a standard brokerage account (defined in Chapter 9), taxes take a giant bite out of your earnings. However, when you invest your money inside a retirement account, like a 401(k) or an IRA, it's like giving your funds an exclusive VIP pass to a backstage tax-free party.

401(k) and IRA retirement accounts act as a protective shield, fending off taxes and safeguarding your money's growth. This unique protection encourages people to save for retirement—to pay themselves first. Aim to save at least 15% of your income for retirement (Ward, 2023). Although you can't tap into the funds until you reach a certain age without facing penalties, consider them a promise to your future self, ensuring you'll have a comfortable, or even luxurious, retirement.

401(k) EMPLOYER-SPONSORED RETIREMENT PLAN

401(k)s are often hailed as the giant golden ticket for working adults to secure their financial future. It's an employer-sponsored plan, meaning you can only participate in a 401(k) if the company you work for includes it in your onboarding packet (Fernando, 2023).

One great thing about 401(k)s is employer matching, where your employer adds a certain percentage of your income to your savings (Tretina, 2023). This feature essentially means you're getting free money. For example, you earn $1,000, and your employer offers a dollar-for-dollar match of up to 5% of your gross income. That's $50, the maximum your employer will contribute for free monthly. If you save $40 from your paychecks, your employer also adds $40, resulting in a total savings of $80. Even if you choose to save $60, you'll still receive the maximum match of $50 because $50 is the limit. However, it doesn't mean you can't save more. You can always save more. Let me repeat: You can always save more.

401(k) employer matching is like icing on the cake, so always shoot to save a portion of your income equal to the match. Unfortunately, as a teen, you may not meet the qualifications to be eligible for a 401(k) (IRS.gov, 2023). However, when you arrive at that point in your career where you're offered a 401(k), seize the opportunity to invest your money. Learn how it works, and sign up for the plan. Note that not all companies offer a 401(k), so take this into account when seeking employment—it's an important factor to consider. And always remember: *Do not leave free money on the table.*

INDIVIDUAL RETIREMENT ACCOUNT

So what's a teen to do now? Enter Individual Retirement Accounts (IRAs)! Like 401(k)s, IRAs allow you to save money for retirement without the taxman taking a bite of your earnings. Unlike 401(k)s, however, employers don't offer IRAs to employees (Kindness, 2023). It's up to individuals to take the initiative and sign up for an IRA. IRAs provide an excellent opportunity for those whose employers don't offer a 401(k) and teenagers who otherwise may not be eligible for a 401(k). It's worth noting that *you can invest in both a 401(k) and an IRA* (Coombes, 2023)—this is huge.

Roth vs. Traditional

There are two types of IRAs relevant to you: Roth and Traditional. Both types offer tax-free growth for your contributions, meaning the money you set aside gets to grow without being affected by taxes (Kindness, 2023). A key distinction between Roth and Traditional lies in the timing of taxation. Roth IRAs require you to pay taxes on your contributions *upfront*, while Traditional IRAs *delay* tax payments until you withdraw funds in retirement (Kindness, 2023). For young earners with lower incomes, the Roth IRA is the clear winner. The decision essentially boils down to taxes, and I'll explain.

Tax Wars

Income earners are categorized into tax brackets such as 10%, 12%, 22%, 24%, etc. (Josephson, 2023). Each bracket represents a range of income, with the lowest earners positioned in the lowest tax bracket. As income increases, individuals move upward to higher tax brackets. Consequently, the tax you pay is determined by the bracket you fall into. As you can see, lower income equates to lower taxes, which is where you currently stand.

Why does this matter? *Paying less taxes means you have more funds to contribute to your Roth IRA for tax-free growth.* And we know that the sooner you get those funds working for you, the better. Now, having paid taxes upfront, you won't ever have to deal with them again when you withdraw your money in retirement (Kindness, 2023) for, you know, that much-deserved vacation with Bestie. Whatever is sitting in your retirement account is entirely yours.

Conversely, as you age and earn more, you'll likely end up in a higher tax bracket. If you opt for a Traditional IRA, you'll postpone taxes to your retirement years (Kindness, 2023). When you withdraw funds for that vacation, expect the tax-man to join you because you haven't paid taxes on your contributions. Whatever is sitting in your retirement account is *not* entirely yours.

Why would some people choose Traditional IRAs if Roth IRAs are considered the clear winner? Firstly, they expect their retirement income to be lower than it currently is, resulting in lower taxes when they withdraw their money (Kindness, 2023). Secondly, Traditional IRAs were the original choice before Roth IRAs came into play (Hartill, 2022).

Thirdly, Traditional IRAs do not have income limits; Roth IRAs do, meaning you can't contribute to a Roth IRA if your income exceeds a certain level (Kindness, 2023).

For you, starting with a Roth IRA makes perfect sense since you're entering the working world fresh and likely at your lowest income, resulting in lower taxes (Bell, 2022). However, transitioning to a Traditional IRA may be necessary as your earnings approach the Roth IRA income limit. In case you become attached to your Roth IRA (as many people do), there's a Backdoor Roth IRA, a legal loophole that allows you to convert from a Traditional IRA to a Roth IRA (Scott, 2023). Don't worry about this for now; it's a consideration for the future. When you reach that point in your financial journey, consider it a good "problem" to have—you're moving up in life and income. Keep up the climb!

Regardless of whether taxes are lower or higher—now or later—choosing a Roth IRA over a Traditional IRA can offer you peace of mind. With a Roth IRA, you can sleep easy, knowing you won't face frequent visits from the taxman during your retirement years. This peace of mind may just override the argument over taxes. Truthfully, we're not sure which tax bracket we'll end up in during retirement, so deciding between a Roth IRA and a Traditional IRA based on our tax predictions decades down the line can create unnecessary uncertainty—food for your thoughts.

8

———— ✕ ————

Unveiling Roth IRAs

I can hear you loud and clear: "A Roth IRA? I'm still studying for my SAT! I'd rather get the inside scoop on SATs. Can you give me that instead?"

Maybe in another book. But listen closely: "You *NEED* a Roth IRA!" It's the single most important thing you need within the context of this book for a shot at your best life in retirement, and *it's something you can have access to right now.*

First, let's reiterate a crucial point: tax-free growth is a very big deal. Remember those pesky paycheck deductions we talked about? Well, imagine handing over a substantial portion of your earnings to the taxman every time your wealth grows in your Roth IRA. Need I say more?

Next, it's a passive income stream through compound interest and dividends (a term we'll discuss later), aligning with the idea of "making money while you sleep."

Then, there's the investment opportunity. Roth IRAs grant you access to the stock market, a crucial element in building and accumulating wealth.

Finally, it provides self-protection. Roth IRAs feature built-in rules that discourage you from prematurely dipping into your funds (Folger, 2023). In a nutshell, Roth IRAs are a direct path to financial security, growing your money exponentially while protecting it from excessive taxes and the risks of self-sabotage. "Self-sabotage" may sound harsh, but it accurately highlights the importance of safeguarding your future.

STARTING WITH A CUSTODIAL ROTH IRA

Doesn't all of this make you want to race off to open a Roth IRA? Except—you must be 18 to open a Roth IRA (Swenson, 2023). No big thing; there's something else just as good—Custodial Roth IRAs. It's mainly a technicality, but the idea is the same. The difference is that your parent or legal guardian will be the one to kickstart opening this account for you (Swenson, 2023). Your job is to convince them to do this; otherwise, you'll have to wait until 18—*so please convince them.*

Under this setup, your parent or legal guardian oversees the account as the *custodian* while you benefit from the growth as the *beneficiary* (Swenson, 2023). You still have a say in your investments, but they'll handle the paperwork and help you manage the account in your best interest. When you turn 18, you'll receive a notification to transfer account ownership to you, your Custodial Roth IRA becomes a Roth IRA, and it'll be all yours for the taking (Swenson, 2023).

The moral of the story? *Grab the Custodial Roth IRA by the horns as soon as you have "earned income."* Take the initiative to talk to your parents about your interest in Roth IRAs and help them grasp why this is such an epic deal for you right now. Discuss the types of investments you're interested in and why. Parents love it when you keep them in the loop— it's like an unwritten rule or something. They'll appreciate your eagerness, and it's an excellent way to prove your maturity. The great thing about Custodial Roth IRAs is that parents (or anyone else) can contribute (Folger, 2023). It's an excellent alternative to them giving you cash for your birthday or holidays, which may otherwise be spent quickly.

Suppose you've hit this 18-year mark. Congratulations! You get to open a Roth IRA all your own. It'll be one of your most significant early adult life experiences. You'll feel so proud of yourself for reaching this financial milestone that you can't help but ooze confidence.

ADHERING TO ROTH IRA RULES

I've emphasized the importance of having "earned income" several times, and now we've arrived at the discussion. Like many organized plans, Roth IRAs come with lengthy rules and regulations. This section will focus on the three essential rules for opening a Roth IRA. This way, you can continue to gain momentum in your investment journey without being overwhelmed and held back by lengthy details. Once you've got the ball rolling and figured out the big kinks, you should trail back and familiarize yourself with some of the nitty gritty. You don't have to absorb all the information at once. Instead, concentrate on the pieces that pertain to the phase in your investment journey.

Here are the three rules to know before you open a Roth IRA:

- Rule #1: To be eligible to contribute to a Roth IRA, you must have "earned income," and taxes must have been paid on those earnings—this means you put in after-tax dollars (Folger, 2023). Money you made from part-time jobs or freelance gigs count as earned income, but gifted money and allowances do not.

- Rule #2: The combined total of your contributions and gifted contributions cannot exceed your earned income (Folger, 2023). For instance, if you earn $5,000 annually, you can contribute $4,000 of your own money, and your parents (or anyone else) can add up to another $1,000. If only $2,000 came from you, then another $3,000 can come from them.

- Rule #3: Your contributions are restricted to an annual limit, which may change from year to year. In 2024, the annual contribution limit is $7,000 for individuals under 50 and $8,000 for those 50 and over (Folger, 2023). So, even if you earned $9,000, you can only put in the maximum of $7,000.

With these three rules in mind, your objective is to maximize your Roth IRA contributions within the allowed limits. Your Roth IRA automatically records your contributions, making it easy to track how much you've saved throughout the year. However, if you inadvertently saved more than the limit, first—good for you, and second, contact your account administrator for assistance as soon as you become aware of it to avoid unnecessary headaches.

"But what if I need to take out some money for something more immediate?"

I understand that life happens, and you may need quick access to cash. Although you can withdraw your contributions before retirement without penalty (O'Shea, 2023), I strongly advise against it. Taking money out before it's time is like taking one step forward and three steps back. What good, then, is this golden ticket? We're talking about your future here, where *nobody's* sending you a paycheck one day—so let's pretend I never mentioned it. That's like telling you not to think of a pink elephant—all you're going to do is think of a pink elephant. Just don't make early withdrawals, okay?

What's the solution, then? You can explore options like getting a second job, reducing your expenses to the bare bones, cutting out unnecessary spending, and doing whatever else it takes to create more cash to get out of your temporary setback. It may seem a little intense, but it's the reality. The key word is "temporary." Hit the pavement, grind your way out of the situation, and get back on track. It'll be tough, but only for a season or two. It'll be tougher if you keep relying on your retirement contributions to fund immediate "needs." Here's another mantra: "Once the money goes in, it stays in."

Let's tie everything together: If you have an emergency fund and sinking funds in place, practice zero-based budgeting, live within your means, steer clear of debt, invest consistently, and master a solid financial mindset, you won't need to take money out of your Roth IRA (or 401(k)). Comprendo? Keep learning and applying financial wisdom; the system will become second nature, allowing you to avoid such a harsh reality. And taking money out will sound insane.

CHOOSING WHERE TO OPEN A ROTH IRA

Many platforms offer Roth IRAs, ranging from local banks to specialized brokerage firms. While signing up for a Roth IRA through your bank may seem convenient, brokerage firms are the superior choice; they provide more investment options, enabling your money to grow faster (Walrack, 2023). It's time to make your money work for you, which means moving it out of your bank and into a brokerage. Otherwise, your money will disappear on stuff that loses value faster than milk goes bad.

A brokerage is like a middleman for your money's ultimate job. Think of it as a marketplace, but instead of fruits, vegetables, or meats, you're shopping around for pieces of different companies and other investments. The brokerage acts as this virtual marketplace, providing the tools, resources, and a platform to buy and sell assets among investors conveniently in one place (O'Shea, 2023). There are numerous brokerages to choose from, and each with unique features and offerings. When selecting a brokerage, consider factors such as ease of use, fees, investment options, research tools, and customer service.

Let's chat about two brokerage heavyweights: Fidelity vs. Vanguard. Why these two? Because they're kind of a big deal in the brokerage world, and many investment gurus consider them among the best places to invest your money (Tretina, 2023). Choosing between the two is like deciding between two different but equally nice cars—both will take you where you need to go, but the ride may feel different.

Although closing your eyes and pointing to a name may be a safe bet, comparing their pros and cons is essential. Details that may align better with your preferences may take time to become apparent, so give it a few rounds. When you're ready to take the plunge into investing, go online and search "Fidelity vs. Vanguard." Online research is usually sufficient for making an informed decision. Take your time and perform multiple searches until information starts to repeat itself.

An excellent starting point is to look into online comparison charts and reviews to determine which aspects matter most to you. Once you narrow that down, dive deeper into those particular aspects. Visit Fidelity's and Vanguard's websites for further details. Contact their customer service and chat with a team member. These brokerages value your business, and they'll gladly assist you in making an informed decision.

Whichever brokerage you select now isn't etched in stone. You can switch brokerages anytime if you change your mind (Haegele, 2023). Brokerages are tools to help you grow your money. If one doesn't do the job the way you like, no rule says you can't switch to the other. I opted not to do a side-by-side comparison of Fidelity and Vanguard since data in the financial world is ever-changing, and any presented here may quickly become outdated. Besides, it's better to obtain such intricate information directly from the source. When choosing between these heavyweights or others, your decision ultimately depends on your preferences, priorities, and investment style.

Practical Exercise: Comparing the Heavyweights
Grab a sheet of paper and create two columns labeled Fidelity and Vanguard. List the pros and cons you've discovered about each. Circle the items that matter the most to you. Your best match will be the column with more circles. Repeat this several times as you gather information.

OPENING A ROTH IRA

Opening a Roth IRA is as simple as 1-2-3 once you decide on a brokerage firm—Fidelity, Vanguard, or any other. Now, having an account set up doesn't mean you're invested. You must take additional steps, such as transferring funds and buying assets; the steps here only prepare you for the excitement that's to come. It doesn't hurt to set up your Roth IRA in advance; Fidelity and Vanguard do not charge inactivity fees (Carey, 2023). But check with others. When you're ready to invest, it's simply a matter of having the necessary funds.

Here are the steps to open your Roth IRA and get it primed up for investing:

1. Open an Account: Visit your chosen brokerage's website, navigate through the tabs, and follow the prompts to open a Roth IRA. Be prepared to provide some personal information.

2. Link Accounts: Connect your bank account(s) to your Roth IRA. Once again, navigate through the tabs and follow the prompts. Have your bank routing number (a financial institution's ID#) and account number handy.

3. Set Up Direct Deposit (optional): Supercharge your savings by arranging direct deposit to your Roth IRA. Decide on the percentage you want to invest each payday and specify that amount on your employer's direct deposit form. Keep your brokerage routing number and account number accessible. This step ensures funds are available for investing.

Your Roth IRA is now set up for investing. When you receive that first paycheck, be sure to allocate some money to your Roth IRA and get those dollars working. Until then, let's get you good and ready! Although investing isn't rocket science, it's complex enough for a quick lesson on the basics before jumping in. Do you know what this means? You'll need to take a crash course on the basics!

9

---∞---

Simplifying Stock Market Jargon

Are you excited to become an investor but worry you'll feel like a fake? Those money people in their suits and ties seem pretty intelligent and intimidating. How could you even call yourself an investor when you look nothing like them? That's the thing. Many believe that investing is only for "those" kinds of people. I'm here to tell you: You don't need to pull off that persona to be an investor. You do, however, need to pull off some investment terminology.

Understanding the language of investing will empower you to become a confident investor—not the suit and tie. Terms like "ROI," "capital gains," and "dividends" may seem just as intimidating as those well-dressed financial experts, but they hold the keys to your financial success, so let's not avoid them. For instance, ROI isn't just an acronym; it measures how profitable your investment is. Capital gains and dividends aren't just payouts but a source of passive income.

This brings us to the crash course. Sink your teeth into the following list of terminology. This one takes the bait as a class assignment—I'm sorry, there's no other way around it. We'll use most of the terms in the following chapter as we dive into investing. So sit up straight, shoulders back, and tackle this jargon confidently. Don't rush through it; you're gearing up for the next stage in your financial journey!

Get some water and come back.

All set?

Let's begin.

Stock Market

The stock market is a virtual space where individuals gather to buy and sell investments, serving as a potent tool for building wealth (Camargo, 2023).

Trade

Trade is the act of buying or selling investments in the stock market (Hayes, 2022).

Stocks

Stocks represent partial ownership in a company (Camargo, 2023). Stocks are actively traded on the stock market during market hours, and their prices fluctuate throughout the day based on various factors (Kennon, 2022).

Shares

Shares are units of stock. When you purchase a unit of a company's stock, you own a share of the company and become a shareholder (Camargo, 2023).

Publicly Traded Company

A publicly traded company allows people to acquire shares of their stock through the stock market (Bowen, 2023).

Ticker Symbol

A ticker symbol is a unique combination of letters that identifies publicly traded assets (Waterworth, 2023). For example, Amazon is AMZN, Target is TGT, and Apple is AAPL.

Asset Class

An asset class is a group of investment types that share similar characteristics, such as stocks and bonds (Brock, 2023).

Bonds

Bonds function as loans to a company or government. When you invest in a bond, you're essentially loaning them money. In return, they promise to repay the initial amount and periodic interest payments as a thank-you (Fontinelle, 2023). This promise makes bonds a safe investment option, ideal for a strategy focused on preserving accumulated wealth (Camargo, 2023). However, bonds offer lower earning potential than stocks (Tretina, 2023).

This distinction is crucial, especially during your younger years, when you should focus on accumulating wealth rather than preserving it (Sinusoid, 2021). As such, bonds take a secondary role in your investment strategy. Stocks (particularly index funds) take the primary role, offering higher earnings and faster wealth accumulation. Bonds will enter the picture much later, becoming more relevant when the focus shifts to preserving wealth for retirement (Camargo, 2023).

Investment Portfolio

An investment portfolio is a collection of asset classes an investor owns (Camargo, 2023).

Diversification

Diversification is a fundamental investment strategy that involves spreading your money across various asset classes to minimize market risk and avoid relying on a single investment (Fidelity, n.d.).

Asset Allocation

Asset allocation is a strategy used alongside diversification that involves determining what percentage of your portfolio will be invested in each asset class (Camargo, 2023). The goal is to create a balanced portfolio that meets your objective while managing risk. For instance, an 80/20 or a 70/30 asset allocation means you have 80% or 70% of your investments in stocks and 20% or 30% in bonds, respectively (Lake, 2022). You can further diversify stocks to include international companies, creating allocations such as 70/20/10 (70% U.S., 20% international, and 10% bonds) (Lake, 2023). Asset allocation can be as simple or complex as one prefers, but we're shooting for simple.

Market Index

A market index acts like a scorecard for companies publicly traded on the stock market. Examples of market indexes are the S&P 500 Market Index and the NASDAQ 100 Market Index. Each index represents a distinct set of companies and provides a numerical snapshot of their overall performance (Camargo, 2023). It's a way for you to see how your investments are doing.

A rise in the S&P 500 Market Index or the NASDAQ 100 Market Index suggests that the companies held inside them are doing better on average than before, and vice versa. If you have investments in any of those companies, their performance moves according to these market indexes. The S&P 500 Market Index is considered the gold standard among market indexes (Brewster, 2023), making it wise to consider investing in an index fund that tracks it.

Mutual Funds

Imagine you and your friends are packing up for a trip, and everyone pitches in some money for snacks. Your friends trust you to choose and buy the snacks, and they're cool with whatever you decide.

Mutual funds operate similarly. They collect money from different people to buy shares of various investments, such as stocks, bonds, and other assets, and when you purchase a share of a mutual fund, you instantly own a portion of all the investments held within that fund in one go (Camargo, 2023). Skilled fund managers actively select what goes into the fund

(Yochim, 2023). The catch is that these skilled fund managers expect compensation for their expertise and active involvement. So, although you get to own a diverse collection of investments all at once, there's a fee to pay—the management fees (Yochim, 2023).

Index Funds

Index funds represent a specific category of mutual funds, operating similarly but with a key distinction. Unlike mutual funds, index funds don't have fund managers actively selecting which companies to include; instead, they *passively* track and replicate a specific market index, such as the S&P 500 Market Index (Yochim, 2023). What does that mean for us? It means we're not paying anyone for their expertise and active involvement. While index funds cost a bit of money to run, they cost significantly less than mutual funds because the active players are out of the equation (Yochim, 2023).

Index funds are traded after the stock market has closed. Although you can place orders to buy shares of index funds during market hours, their prices are determined at the end of the trading day, at which point orders are automatically fulfilled at that price (Fidelity, n.d.).

Exchange-Traded Funds (ETFs)

ETFs function similarly to index funds, holding a collection of investments and tracking market indexes (Fidelity, n.d.).

However, the difference lies in their trading behavior. While index funds are traded after market hours at a single price, ETFs are traded during market hours, with fluctuating prices (Fidelity, n.d.). You can specify your price, and your orders are automatically executed when your target price is reached.

Expense Ratio (ER)

ER measures a fund's operating cost, so the lower the ER, the better (Royal, 2023). Passively managed index funds and ETFs generally come with lower expense ratios than actively managed mutual funds (Tretina, 2023), making them our preferred investment choice.

Compound Interest

By now, you already know what compound interest is—the magic trick. But we can't have a terminology section without including compound interest. So, imagine you have a money tree that grows yearly based on the previous year's growth. If you had $1,000 on your money tree this year and it grows by 10%, you'll have $1,100 next year. The year after that, it doesn't just grow by 10% of your initial $1,000; it grows by 10% of the $1,100 you had last year, and you end up with $1,210. The pattern repeats. See how it's like a snowball rolling downhill, getting bigger and bigger?

There's a mathematical formula for compound interest. Look it up if you're curious to see how it works. But it's enough to know that compounding can occur daily, monthly, quarterly, semi-annually, or annually, depending on the type of investment (Fernando, 2023). The more frequently interest is compounded, the more your investment will grow.

Dividends

Remember the four reasons why you need a Roth IRA? One of them was passive income through dividends. When companies generate profits or positive cash flow, they distribute some to their shareholders as dividends (Camargo, 2023). By investing in a company's stock, you get money when they make money. You read that right. You do nothing, and they pay you. The more shares you have, the more you get paid. You can use the money you earn from dividends to reinvest and buy more shares (Royal, 2023). Before you know it, you'll be looking at a nice chunk of cash growing all on its own.

Return on Investment (ROI)

ROI measures how profitable an investment is; it gauges whether you're gaining more from your investment than you initially put in (Fernando, 2023). If you invest $10 and end up with $20, your ROI is 100%, indicating that your investment is performing well. A positive ROI is free money.

Capital Gains

Capital gains are the profits you earn when you sell assets at a higher price than you initially paid (Camargo, 2023). Short-term capital gains occur when assets are sold within a year, while long-term capital gains are applied to assets held for over a year. This distinction is important because short-term capital gains are generally taxed at a higher rate than long-term capital gains (IRS.gov, 2023). So, it's wiser to keep investments for over a year. However, tax implications and holding periods are not a concern when investing inside a retirement account. Remember the tax-free party? Short-term and long-term capital gains taxes typically apply to those who invest in standard brokerage accounts.

Standard Brokerage Account

A standard brokerage account is your flexible go-to investment account. You can invest in the stock market and access your money anytime without penalties, but the catch is you'll need to pay capital gains tax every time you sell assets for more than you paid (Folger, 2023).

Retirement Brokerage Account

A retirement brokerage account is your investment's tax-free haven. While you can also invest in the stock market, the beauty is that you *won't* incur tax on your capital gains when you sell assets within the account (Dehan, 2023). Why? Because the government wants to reward you for saving for retirement. The catch? You'll face penalties and taxes if you take out your earnings before a certain age (Folger, 2023). But it's a protective measure that turns into a win-win situation.

Here's a little secret: One day, you can have both. When you reach a point in your career where you're able to max out your 401(k) and IRA retirement accounts, you can invest extra money into a standard brokerage account. That way, you'll enjoy flexibility *and* security! A great day!

We've reached the end of the terminology chapter. It wasn't so bad, right? Every party has a dull moment, so let's call this one it. Don't be discouraged if you don't grasp some of the terms. Every expert was once a beginner. Soon, you'll speak this language so fluently that it'll flow off your tongue. Since you're still here, go ahead and run through the list once more (oh, come on). Then, we'll move on.

Done with round two?

As you level up in Chapter 10, refer to this chapter if you forget the meaning of specific terms.

10

---∞---

Mastering Index Funds

B y now, your brain is fired up, and you understand that investing is the one crucial step you must take to build long-term wealth. You've learned about 401(k)s and IRAs, the two big golden tickets leading to a comfortable and secure retirement. You've gained insights into why the Roth IRA option makes sense for you and now know how to open an account through a brokerage. With a recent crash course in investment terminology under your belt, we're closing the loop. You're about to learn precisely how to invest within your Roth IRA, and you're not just a step closer to creating the life of your dreams—you're strutting straight through the double doors. Can you picture yourself, head held high? It's a significant moment. Investing at such a young age is an achievement to be *proud* of.

Investing for your future isn't some glamorous event happening on the sidelines of your life—it's mundane, and it should be. Leave the glitz and glamour for Hollywood; we'll take crickets. But seriously, when you're playing with your money, you'd want to keep things at cruise control. That way, you can take your foot off the pedal and focus on your destination. You may get sidetracked if you hear friends talking about the next big stock or how they're making a quick buck. Ignore all that noise. That's not our game. Our game is *index funds—the crème de la crème, the bread and butter, the cornerstone and summit of your Roth IRA.* Soon, your friends will come to you for investing advice.

We touched on index funds in the previous chapter. Let's zoom in for a closer look and get to know them better—to understand the *why* behind investing in them. Then, we'll move on to the step-by-step. I'll break down the concepts into digestible segments to ensure a smoother learning experience and that you stay with me.

Index Funds: The Term
Index funds are a type of investment fund, either a mutual fund or an exchange-traded fund (ETF), designed to closely mirror the performance of a specific market index, such as the S&P 500 Market Index, the NASDAQ 100 Market Index, or the Dow Jones Industrial Average (Yochim, 2023) Market Index. Okay, that didn't help. Let's break it down.

Index Funds: Simplified

Index funds are a type of investment that makes investing in the stock market easy, even if you know nothing about picking individual stocks. Instead of trying to pick winners, an index fund invests your money in a collection of companies all at once. It does this by copying a specific group of stocks known as a market index, such as the S&P 500 Market Index, NASDAQ 100 Market Index, or Dow Jones Industrial Average Market Index.

These market indexes fluctuate every day based on different things happening in the economy. When you invest in an index fund that tracks a specific market index, like the S&P 500 Market Index, your investments go up and down with that market index. Remember, *the index fund itself isn't the market index*—it's simply a way for you to invest in a bunch of companies that make up the market index. So, when you invest in, say, the Fidelity S&P 500 Index Fund (FXAIX), you're essentially investing in the companies that make up the S&P 500 Market Index.

Why Invest in Index Funds: Diversification and Low Risk

Index funds offer instant diversification (Levy, 2023). When you invest in an index fund, you're spreading your money across many companies. If one doesn't perform well, it won't impact your money much because the others balance things out, making index funds a low-risk investment (Levy, 2023).

Why Invest in Index Funds: Passive and Low Fees

Index funds operate on a passive management strategy, aiming to replicate a market index, meaning there is no active involvement of fund managers in selecting which stocks to buy and sell (Levy, 2023). This passive approach keeps the fees for index funds nice and low (Levy, 2023).

Why Invest in Index Funds: Putting It All Together

Index funds check all the major boxes for building wealth—they're low-cost, passive, diversified, and low-risk. Even better, you don't have to monitor them as you would if you had hand-picked individual stocks (Gravler, 2023). All you need to do is add money to your index fund and let it do the heavy lifting. It's an easy, hassle-free way to build wealth while saving time and energy (Gravler, 2023).

Why Invest in Index Funds: Buffett's Recommendation

Have you ever heard of Warren Buffett? He's *only* regarded as one of the most successful investors of the 20th century. Well, he's got a message for all of us: *Invest in an S&P 500 Index Fund* (Speights, 2023). Feel free to share this with Bestie.

What's an S&P 500 Index Fund?

An S&P 500 Index Fund closely mirrors the S&P 500 Market Index, including 500 of the largest U.S. companies (Bloomenthal, 2023), such as Coca-Cola, Microsoft, Amazon, and Tesla. When you buy a single share of an S&P 500 Index Fund, you get instant access to a diversified portfolio that includes these 500 companies. Not only is it diversified, but it's also passive, low-cost, low-risk, and requires minimal effort. (Bloomenthal, 2023). Getting the idea?

S&P 500 Index Fund vs. Total Stock Market Index Fund

Do you remember how the titans of brokerages Fidelity and Vanguard compete head-to-head? Index funds do the same thing. An S&P 500 Index Fund is often compared to a Total Stock Market Index Fund (Success with Money, 2023). While the S&P 500 Index Fund represents the 500 largest U.S. companies, the Total Stock Market Index Fund represents the entire U.S. stock market, including a broader range of small, medium, and large-sized companies (Thune, 2022). Despite this difference, these index funds perform similarly (Thune, 2022)—so similarly that if you can't seem to decide between them, I'd say leave it to Eeny, Meeny, Miny, and Moe. You know what I mean. Essentially, both index funds will do the job—to build long-term wealth.

Index Funds vs. ETFs

Let's talk about another investment showdown: Index Funds vs. ETFs. As mentioned earlier, both index funds and ETFs follow market indexes but differ mainly in their trading style. ETFs allow you to shop for desired prices during market hours, while index funds provide a single price after the market closes (Fidelity, n.d.).

ETFs seem like they have an edge because they offer the flexibility to select your desired price. While that's a valid point, let's revisit our fundamental investing goal and apply some critical thinking. We aim to start investing as soon as possible and stay invested for the long term, no matter what happens to short-term price fluctuations. We want to harness the power of time and the magic of compound interest. So, the price at which we place our trades shouldn't matter much throughout our investment journey. What matters more is placing those trades consistently and continuously. Prices can move up, down, or sideways—and that's okay.

The stock market is intricate, and constantly trying to time the market with ETFs can be stressful. It can also consume time that could be better spent elsewhere. The idea of having an "edge" may tempt people to wait for the "perfect time," but in reality, there's no such edge, and there's no perfect time (Loudenback, 2020). That's why index funds make more investment sense from a psychological standpoint as well as an objective standpoint.

Start With ETFs and End With Index Funds

There's a scenario where ETFs may be the better choice. Some brokerages like Vanguard require a higher initial investment for their index funds than ETFs (Vanguard, n.d.). Thus, if you don't have much money to invest, ETFs may be your first choice (Burns, 2023). You can switch to index funds later.

The Deciding Factor

If you're especially eager to invest your money into index funds from the start, consider Fidelity, where there are no minimum investment requirements for index funds (Tetrina, 2023). It could be the deciding factor between the duo Fidelity and Vanguard.

Principles Over Specifics

Regardless of your brokerage or fund type choice, your goal is to invest in a diversified fund, spreading risk while aiming for a competitive return. It's worth remembering this principle when your employer presents you with a 401(k) opportunity. While companies strive to offer a variety of funds, their 401(k) plans may have limitations compared to the broader fund options available in IRAs (Prinzel, 2023). For instance, your company may not include funds with specific titles like S&P 500 Index Fund or U.S. Total Stock Market Index Fund. However, you'll likely find investment choices that satisfy the same objective within the available options. Understand that it's more important to grasp the principle than fixate on specific funds.

INVESTING IN INDEX FUNDS

Having laid the groundwork for index funds investing, you now understand the *why* and the *what* behind them. Let's get into the *how*. It'll be so easy that you may find yourself saying, "Wait, that's it?" After all, you've already done the challenging part: grasping the principles and concepts of investing, selecting a suitable brokerage, and identifying an appropriate investment type.

Remember the earlier discussion about opening a Roth IRA? Investing in index funds is an extension of that process. I've reiterated those steps below. But before the step-by-step, you must choose your competition winners. Well, they're all winners—that's why they go head-to-head, but you must still make the hard decision. If you've already set up your Roth IRA—nice!—you're one competition down.

Here are the matchups again:

- Fidelity vs. Vanguard
- S&P 500 Index Fund vs. Total Stock Market Index Fund
- Index Funds vs. ETFs

Having declared your winners, you can still switch them up anytime. Recall that your brokerage is not set in stone and your investments aren't taxed within a retirement account, which means if you sell your initial choice to buy the other and happen to earn a profit, you won't have to worry about incurring capital gains tax. Nevertheless, it's best to make a firm, thought-out decision.

Ready to invest?

Here's the step-by-step:

1. Open an Account: Visit your chosen brokerage's website, navigate through the tabs, and follow the prompts to open a Roth IRA. Be prepared to provide some personal information.

2. Link Accounts: Connect your bank account(s) to your Roth IRA. Once again, navigate through the tabs and follow the prompts. Have your bank routing number and account number handy.

3. Wait for Funds to Settle: It may take up to three business days for your transferred funds to settle, which means your funds have landed in your Roth IRA. Monitor your account balance or wait for a notification.

4. Research: Look up some index funds offered on your brokerage site. Review the fees, fund descriptions, past performances, and covered industries. Avoid overanalyzing; the choices can be overwhelming, and too much analysis can lead to paralysis—analysis paralysis. For starters, focus your research on the S&P 500 Index Fund and the Total Stock Market Index Fund. And let's not forget Warren Buffett's golden nugget of advice from earlier: *Invest in an S&P 500 Index Fund* (Speights, 2023).

Now, here are a few ticker symbols to note:

FXAIX: Fidelity S&P 500 Index Fund
FSKAX: Fidelity Total Stock Market Index Fund
VFIAX: Vanguard S&P 500 Index Fund
VTSAX: Vanguard Total Stock Market Index Fund

5. Place a Trade: When you feel confident, sign into your Roth IRA, locate the Trade tab, and enter the name or ticker symbol of your chosen index fund. Click Buy, specify the dollar amount or number of shares, and click Confirm. Voila! You're officially an investor!

6. Set Up Direct Deposit (optional): Supercharge your savings by arranging direct deposit to your Roth IRA. Decide on the percentage you want to invest each payday and specify that amount on your employer's direct deposit form. Keep your brokerage routing number and account number accessible. This step ensures funds are readily available for investing.

7. Automate Investments (optional): Maximize your savings by setting up automatic transfers and investments in your Roth IRA. Determine the amount, frequency, and index fund you want to invest. Your brokerage takes care of the rest on the specified date, automatically transferring the designated amount from your bank account into your Roth IRA and investing in your chosen index fund. If you've set up direct deposit, your funds

are already available for automatic investments. In this case, you don't need to transfer money from your bank first; your brokerage will proceed directly to the investment part. This process guarantees consistent contributions to your future with every paycheck.

8. Check-In: Occasionally check on your investment, more out of curiosity than anything else. Whether it's up or down, don't think much of it. This investment style is designed to be simple, effective, and stress-free. You're not dabbling in individual stocks, day trading (the risky buying and selling of investments to make quick profits), timing the market, or lacking diversification. You're checking in, checking out, and moving on.

9. Keep Investing: Your journey has just begun. Regularly add to your investments. Even small, seemingly insignificant contributions can grow significantly, thanks to the power of compound interest and time. Always remember: The stock market fluctuates but trends upward, and view market dips as a sale and an opportunity to buy more with less (Daly, 2023).

LEVELING UP YOUR INDEX FUNDS INVESTING

You've just executed your first trade. Now what? As a long-term investor beginning at this early stage, your investment approach should remain simple, consistent, and pretty much hands-off: Invest in a single diversified index fund and keep adding to it. There's no need to contemplate changing this approach for quite a while—as in years or even decades.

At that point, you may consider adding a second or a third fund to your portfolio, adjusting your asset allocation away from a one-fund portfolio to a two-fund or a three-fund portfolio (Kumok, 2023). Remember the 80/20 and 70/20/10 asset allocation models? You can slice and dice them however you like, say 90/10, 95/5, 80/15/5, or 85/10/5. Although adding additional funds to your portfolio is an option you can consider anytime, it's important to remember that it isn't necessary to invest in multiple funds, especially when you're just starting or want to keep it manageable (Curry, 2023).

The challenge with needlessly breaking up your portfolio into parts is that you must periodically rebalance your investments to maintain your desired allocation, which involves selling well-performing investments to buy underperforming ones, among other things (Heyford, 2023). You may not have time to focus on this as you transition from high school to college to a big-time career. Remember, investing for long-term wealth should be passive, not busywork. You want to spend your precious time doing other meaningful things. You know, like planning your Sweet 16, preparing for your learner's permit, or traveling to the finals.

The beauty of beginning your investment journey at a young age and staying committed for the long term is that you don't need to obsess over finding the perfect asset allocation mix or exact funds that will earn you the highest returns. Contemplating the "ideal" asset allocation mix or funds becomes irrelevant when sticking to a single fund does the job just fine and when you have decades for the stock market to run its course. Keep it simple and consistent, and resist the urge to chase minor differences in gains. Imagine leaving a store, and a competitor down the street pings you a 5% discount code for an item you've just purchased. Would you get back in line to return that item and drive down the street? *A millionaire is a millionaire; financial freedom is financial freedom.*

Once you've accumulated significant wealth, you may consider adding a bond fund to your portfolio to preserve the wealth gained through your stock fund(s) (Camargo, 2023). You have a lot of time to familiarize yourself with these concepts before making such decisions. However, if you want to add a bond fund (or an international fund) now, it's your call—there's no one-size-fits-all. Choose the approach that suits your preferences, situation, and time frame, and do so with investment knowledge and sensibility. Search Google, read up on the potential best mixes for different age groups and scenarios, and make an informed decision. Take your time; investing is a journey, not a destination. And Rome wasn't built in a day, you know. But it was built to last.

Keeping those principles in mind, let's explore how to easily level up your investment journey. Let's build Rome.

Leveling Up Through a One-Fund Portfolio

Imagine investing your money in only a single diversified index fund and witnessing it substantially grow your wealth over time. That's what maintaining a one-fund portfolio can accomplish—the concept we've just discussed. With the average annual return of the major U.S. stock market indexes (e.g., S&P 500 Market Index or Total Stock Market Index) over the last 50 years being approximately 10% (Mitchell, 2023), sticking to a single U.S. stock index fund that tracks these market indexes could take you far. Use a compound interest calculator to see how. Explore the potential returns on different investment amounts with an average 10% return and start dreaming about your future.

Implementing a one-fund portfolio is as easy as 1) selecting an index fund, either one tracking the S&P 500 Market Index or one tracking the Total Stock Market Index (or something similar), and 2) continuing to purchase more shares of that single fund. That's it! You've just taken your investing to the next level. There's no need to constantly monitor individual stock prices or manage multiple funds. As a busy young investor balancing school and work, you'll appreciate a one-fund portfolio's streamlined and straightforward nature. You've got junior prom to plan! Or senior ball.

Leveling Up Through Dollar-Cost Averaging

You may now realize that investing should be a year-round commitment, regardless of stock market conditions. There's a name for that—Dollar-Cost Averaging (DCA), and it's the one-fund portfolio's special sidekick. DCA strategy involves consistently investing the same amount of money at regular intervals, regardless of price, year-round (Hayes, 2023).

Suppose you invest $100 monthly in the Fidelity S&P 500 Index Fund (FXAIX). In certain months, $100 will buy you more shares when prices are lower. In other months, it will buy you fewer shares when prices are higher. Over time, this approach averages out the cost per share, resulting in an overall price that may be lower than if you had purchased all your shares at once at a higher-than-average price (Hayes, 2023). The idea behind DCA is more about consistency than the exact dollar amount. In other words, you can invest $100 five months in a row and $50 in the sixth month if $50 is all you have—it's not all or nothing. If you have $200 in the seventh month, do $200—even better.

By eliminating the need to monitor stock prices, DCA offers a simple and efficient investment style, encouraging investors to keep investing (Hayes, 2023). That said, don't feel you must stick exclusively to DCA. If you have a lump sum, you can throw it all in if you want. Get them in; get them going. Nothing is stopping you from incorporating both methods.

Leveling Up Through Reinvested Dividends

You've just met the one-fund portfolio's special sidekick, DCA. Meet its other special sidekick: dividends—not just any dividends but *reinvested dividends*. Dividends are like little cash rewards companies give their shareholders when they turn a profit (Camargo, 2023). When they make money, you make money. It's their way of saying thank you for taking a chance and investing in their company.

Companies have a predefined schedule for distributing dividends, and you'll see those funds get deposited directly into your Roth IRA (Beers, 2023). You can cash them out, or here's where the magic happens—you can reinvest them. Now that you're an investor, can you guess which choice is wiser? Yes, *reinvest them*. You're getting a good hang of this. *Reinvesting your dividends is like giving compound interest and DCA a turbo boost,* or like earning extra credit on extra credit.

Compound interest in action: When you reinvest dividends, you're using the reinvested dividends to buy more shares of the same investment. These additional shares then generate their dividends. Over time, this compounding significantly increases your wealth. But wait, that's only your dividends compounding. The rest of your money is also pumping out its compounding magic on the back end. We could talk about the snowball effect here (or the money pet zoo or the drum solo), but I think you get it.

DCA in action: When you reinvest dividends, you're essentially dollar-cost averaging (Royal, 2023). You're not trying to time the market; you're simply adding more money to your investments whenever you have it. Except—you're using dividends (free money!).

Reinvesting dividends doesn't require active decision-making. It's automatic once you set it up. When you set up your automatic investments (Step 8), you can set up automatic reinvesting dividends at that time.

Leveling Up Through Time

Some people think investing is about waiting for that golden opportunity, as if hundreds of stars will suddenly align and glow a bright neon sign saying, "Invest Now!" While they're waiting for this magical moment to appear, something more precious slips away—time. Time is the real gold here. It's not about figuring out the best time to enter the market. It's about getting into the market *now.* There's this saying in the investing world: "It's about time *in* the market—not about timing the market" (White, 2022).

Picture yourself planting a seed. If you wait for the perfect weather conditions, you may never plant that seed. But if you plant it right away and let it endure the seasons, it will grow. It won't grow overnight, but it will grow. Your investments won't grow overnight, but they *will* grow.

Here's another way to see it. Waiting to time the market is like waiting to score a home run in baseball. You hold off for the perfect pitch that will allow you to knock the ball out of the park. Meanwhile, someone consistently hitting singles and doubles is already circling the bases. They're making progress. And they're scoring. What looks like a better game strategy to you—holding off for the dream pitch or getting into the game and making consistent plays?

Leveling Up Through the No-Panic Approach

What if the market crashes? First, don't panic. Second, don't sell (Daly, 2023). Markets have their ups and downs, kind of like ocean tides. Sure, a market downturn could mean your investment's value may go into dip mode for an undetermined length of time, but that's okay. Historically, markets have consistently bounced back (Ameriprise Investment Research, 2023). Since you're investing for the long haul, these ups and downs won't matter much over time. Your money will continue to grow.

The biggest mistake one can make is selling investments (out of fear) when the stock market takes a downturn. *Selling your shares locks in your losses permanently* (Daly, 2023); essentially, you bought high and sold low. You can't build wealth like that. However, if you do nothing, no matter what, you retain ownership of those shares. When the stock market eventually rebounds, so will the value of your investments (Daly, 2023).

I'm about to scream: *"WHEN THE MARKET GOES DOWN, BUY!"* Stock prices are lower than usual; it's a prime time to get in while it's hot (Daly, 2023). Get this?

There you have it. That's how you level up your investing game. To summarize, begin investing when you're young (leveling up through time) and consistently invest, regardless of stock market conditions (leveling up through the no-panic approach). Even with only small amounts, steadily and gradually grow your investment (leveling up through a one-fund portfolio) from month to month (leveling up through DCA) with automatic reinvestments (leveling up through re-invested dividends). *It's this strategy that builds wealth.*

A Glimpse Into Your Future

Before we transition from the topic of investing, let me paint a vivid picture for you. Imagine you start a part-time job during your sophomore year, clocking in a reasonable 20 hours a week, plus extra hours during summer break. Every hard-earned penny goes into your Roth IRA. Fast forward to the end of your senior year, and you've managed to tuck away $12,000. Awesome job! But there's more.

Now, imagine you make no further efforts to save, and in the hustle and bustle of life, you forget about this money. Fast forward 45 years—you're tired of your daily grind. And out of sheer exhaustion, you suddenly remember your Roth IRA.

You curiously log into your old account, and to your absolute astonishment, you discover a colossal $874,685.80 quietly sitting in your account, waiting for you (Investor.gov, n.d.).

Let this extraordinary reality sink in. Your initial $12,000, at a 10% annual average return rate, has grown into this massive sum while you were busy carrying on with your life. Through the power of the stock market, the magic of compound interest combined with the gift of time, and the sheer genius of letting your money work for you, your life has now turned right-side up.

Your money grew even though you forgot about it. It kept growing even though you didn't add another penny. The power of compounding works silently but astonishingly, turning a forgotten experience into a sigh of relief.

My friend, embrace the potential of investing, and you'll reap the rewards beyond your imagination. As you work hard for your money with sweat and tears, let your money work hard for you. *Allow it to do what it does best—to secure your future.*

11

---∞---

Approaching Credit Cards

Everyone, even the little kids and toddlers, knows what a credit card looks like and how it's used. Load up, swipe, and done—got the goods. But what's really happening behind this simple process? We're about to pull back the curtains on a topic that often leads to heated discussions and the classic phrase, "Let's agree to disagree."

What Is Credit?

Three words: borrow, buy, repay. When you apply for credit, you're asking to borrow money upfront through your bank. Once approved, you don't get real money. You get a plastic card containing a certain amount of points or credits—this is your credit limit, your financial guardrail. You can then use these credits to pay for anything you want up to your credit limit. However, at the end of the spending cycle, your bank expects you to repay the "money" you borrowed in the form of *real* money. When this reality sinks in, many people are too afraid to face it—they don't have *real* money to pay back the bank. That's why, my friend, you must truly understand the backstory of credit cards before even thinking about getting your hands on one. They can quickly become more of a problem than a solution, so approach them with caution.

A credit limit is not an open invitation to indulge in a spending spree. Instead, it's the maximum amount you can borrow. Although some banks permit you to exceed your credit limit, they're not doing it as a favor. You'll face consequences such as declined transactions, increased minimum payments, or a big hit to your credit score (Rathner, 2023).

What's a Credit Score?

A credit score is a three-digit number that reflects your creditworthiness (Brock, 2023). Are you able to repay what you borrowed? Do you pay in full and on time? If so, you're considered creditworthy, and you earn a high score—Woohoo! (maybe). The higher the score, the greater your creditworthiness. But what does that high score mean? It means banks can trust you to repay borrowed money, and when you request more, they'll likely approve it almost instantly (Brock, 2023). With a few clicks, your bank can quickly look up your credit score and determine how much more they'll lend you.

The reverse is true. Your bank can completely deny that request with the same clicks. Your credit score moves according to your payment history (Depersio, 2023). When you're not managing your spending and repayments as well as your bank likes, your score takes a hit. When you improve and get back on track, your score creeps back up—it's scary how the score follows you. This score-tracking system leads many individuals to chase a high score. It's like your financial GPA; the higher the score, the "better." But chasing this high score to gain creditworthiness can be dangerous, as you'll see why.

In an era where information is so accessible, there are better ways to establish your creditworthiness without the risk of spiraling into debt. Consistently paying your bills on time is one such apparent method. That's a significant factor in determining your credit score anyway. Who cares if it may take banks longer than just a few clicks to evaluate your payment history and credit score—they can still do it. So, let's not fall too quickly for the "it's great for your credit score" hype. Apologies for the rant.

Ears open: You only need to worry about a credit score if you rely on debt to fund your lifestyle—*this* must be said. If you opt for a path where you manage your life with *real* money, then there's no need to bother with credit cards and credit scores. They won't even be relevant if you budget, save for short-term and long-term goals, and invest for the future.

147

What's APR?

Annual Percentage Rate—the dream killer. APR measures how much it will cost to borrow money if you don't pay off your balance in full (Stinson, 2023). You see the percentages on your credit card agreement and may think, "Oh, 20% doesn't sound too bad." Wait—it adds up faster than you'd think. Swipe here, tap there, and before you know it, you're shelling out more money in interest and late fees than you ever borrowed. That's not a situation you want to be in. It's the equivalent of sinking in financial quicksand, and trust me, the escape rope isn't cheap. So, always—always—pay off your credit card balance on time, every time.

This takes us back to budgeting. I want to reiterate the crucial benefit of budgeting: It allows you to see where your money will go *before* it starts to go. So, if you own a credit card, "credit card repayment" must be listed in your budget. Allocate a specific amount to your debt repayment, and *do not* use your credit card beyond this monthly limit. If you don't have the cash allocated in your planned budget at the beginning of the month to pay off the entire amount owed when it's due, what makes you think you'll have the cash at the end of the month? I know it may seem intuitive, but when it comes to credit cards, intuitive thinking often goes out the door.

You'll have future credit card cycles, so it's wiser to wait (delay gratification) for the following cycle to make purchases than accumulate interest and fees for not paying the entire amount on the current bill. That APR is always ready to kill your dreams; don't let it. By spreading your spending out between cycles and keeping your credit below your budgeted limit, you can avoid the financial quicksand and become a disciplined manager of your money.

Responsible Usage

While the standard age requirement for applying for a credit card is 18, some banks offer the option of becoming an authorized user on a parent's account (Taylor, 2023). The idea is that you can start learning how to use a credit card responsibly and build credit under the guidance of an adult without being held fully accountable for your actions. Nevertheless, it's not a free pass to be careless; you should still use it as if it were solely your responsibility. But who's to say your parents are even handling it responsibly? (Sorry, parents.)

Your first credit card is more than a financial rite of passage. It marks the beginning of your credit history—a recorded account of everything you've ever done with credit. When you use your credit card wisely and build up a good history, it can become a tool that opens doors—literally. Want to rent your first apartment? Buy a first car? These doors swing wide open. However, misuse your credit card and develop a bad history, and these doors slam shut. The path ahead may be difficult, all from misusing what's supposed to be for "good."

MONEY SKILLS FOR TEENS

Bottom line, credit cards aren't inherently bad. When used responsibly, they may help you attain a certain level of financial independence. But with great power comes great responsibility. If you decide to own a credit card, *use it wisely*, as if carefully weighing each step as you cross a tattered bridge. One wrong move and it can be a life-long struggle. My point is to encourage you to think critically. How can you avoid the common pitfalls and still enjoy the "benefits" of a credit card?

AVOIDING THE CREDIT CARD TRAP

What's the first thing that comes to mind about credit cards? Easy shopping? Opportunities? Quick Loans? What if I told you they're not as cool as they seem? They're almost like that attractive flame that draws innocent moths near—interest rates. Those sneaky, hardly even noticeable interest rates can quickly snowball into an avalanche. And you're trapped. Compound interest is working *against* you here. These cards are plastic, but their impact on your life can feel as hefty as a lead ball. Let's peel back the curtains.

Behind the Curtains

The entire credit card system plays psychological tricks, from how statements are presented to how minimum payments are calculated. These tricks keep you paying them back just enough while trapping you in debt for as long as possible.

Suppose you treat yourself to a shiny new smartphone, and without much thought, you charge the entire amount to your credit card, setting you back $1,000. When the monthly statement arrives, the minimum payment due is only $25. You say to yourself, "No sweat." Just a minute. At an average annual interest rate of 21% (Shultz, 2023), sticking only to the minimum payments means you'll end up paying much more than the original cost of $1,000. What do you think is happening behind the curtains with the remaining $975? Let me tell you: It's racking up interest daily until you clear the debt. So, although you dutifully paid the required amount, you'll still get dinged by your bank. It's that 21% dream killer lurking in the fine print of your credit card statement.

To put it in perspective, 21% of a $975 balance is $204.75. So, here's where it gets dangerous: You make a $25 payment this month, and by next month, your balance will have ballooned to $1,179.75. What was the cost of that smartphone again? Imagine continuing to make the same $25 minimum payment (because your bank is "so generous" and wants to give you some slack). How on earth would you ever escape that initial $1,000 debt? You won't! *They've got you.*

The example simplifies interest calculations, but in the credit world, interest compounds, turning this scenario from bad to worse. It's like tossing your hard-earned cash into a bonfire, bit by bit. As if interest isn't enough, the fees start to pile up.

How long does it take to get rid of that debt? Years. While you struggle to chip away at the interest, you could have invested that money elsewhere, enabling it to grow through the power of compound interest working *for* you, not against you. Each day you delay paying off your credit card debt is another day wasted on earned interest payments. With each tick of the clock, your financial freedom slips further away. Do you want to be shackled with this burden for years? The constant stress of monthly payments looming above your head isn't worth the fleeting thrill of instant gratification— like that shiny smartphone.

When it comes to credit cards, the idea of responsible usage isn't as straightforward as we'd like. What's straightforward is that credit card debt is a financial sinkhole that's way easier to fall into than climb out of. Sure, everyone says, "I'll only use it for emergencies," but human behavior is inconsistent. With the odds stacked against you, those designer glasses on a 30% off sale soon become an "emergency." Then, out of nowhere, you're dealing with your self-imposed emergency. Whatever happened to an emergency fund anyway?

Benefits or Consequences?

Let's cut to the chase—credit card companies aren't running a charity. They're in it to make money. How do they do that? By dangling incentives such as "Swipe for rewards, earn cash back, and build your credit score!" Sounds tempting, right?

However, beneath the surface, these "benefits" often lure you into a perpetual cycle of repayments, where your spending far outweighs the rewards or cashback you earn. As far as building a credit score, you've already seen how chasing a high score can be very dangerous.

I get it. Life's pretty fast-paced, and the convenience of swiping a credit card and the promise of its "benefits" is enticing. Still, be very cautious when something is overly promoted. But cold, hard cash—it requires no sales pitch. It's tangible, universally understood, with no hidden fine print. It's just as convenient, yet its benefits are incomparable.

To be fair, credit cards aren't the spawn of some financial evil; it's in the way they're used. The key to preventing them from becoming problematic is knowing when to use your credit card and when to keep it tucked away in your pocket— a concept called *credit utilization ratio*, which measures the proportion of credit you use compared to your credit limit (Barroso, 2023). Ideally, you should aim to keep this ratio below 30%. For instance, if your credit limit is $10,000, keep your balance below $3,000; doing so signals to lenders that you're not overly desperate for credit, making you more appealing to them if you ever need financial assistance. But would you even need financial assistance? Maybe not if you've mastered the art of money management—it's the goal of this book anyway.

What I'm driving at is the idea that control is essential. The thin line between reaping benefits and wrestling with consequences hinges on whether you take firm control or let it slip away. When you use your credit card, you naturally give away a measure of that control. Claim your financial freedom—think twice before committing to that double-edged credit card. Setting stringent rules and limitations is *crucial* if you decide to sign your name on the dotted line.

The point here is to foster some critical thinking. Are credit cards as cool as they seem? Well, that's for you to decide. But here's my two cents: As you enter the financial arena, don't simply follow the crowd—question, think, and then determine what works best *for you*. How can you enjoy the "perks" of credit cards while sidestepping hidden mines? For me—and this is where we can agree to disagree—I don't like the thought of hidden mines, so I'm sticking with cash. Plus, I've never witnessed any arguments over its usage.

CARRYING ON WITHOUT A CREDIT SCORE

You're scrolling through TikTok or hanging out with friends, and someone brings up the subject of credit scores. Suddenly, you're bombarded with statements such as, "You need to get your credit score up to get a decent car," or "You know you'll never rent an apartment without one, right?" Typical.

Why does society have an obsession with credit scores? Well, society treats credit scores like report cards for adults. Banks, car loan agencies, and mortgage brokers see your credit score as a numerical shorthand for trustworthiness. But that's all that it is—a shortcut. As mentioned, there are other ways to prove your creditworthiness, such as consistently paying all your bills on time, something you should default to anyway. So, remember that you don't owe these institutions anything in exchange for a measly credit score, especially not during your teen years. You're in a transformative phase where you can and *should* prioritize learning about money management over obsessing about a number you don't need.

"What about when I enter the real world?"

I get you. But here's the thing: Financial literacy is your bedrock. A credit score is a flimsy house of cards built on that foundation; it's not the be-all and end-all.

I'm sure your parents or teachers have told you that learning the rules of the game is more important than the score. Financial life is no different. When you focus on mastering the basics of budgeting, saving, investing, and debt avoidance, you're setting yourself up for all-around success. Then, you can navigate the adult world without becoming dependent on a system that wants to commodify your worth down to a three-digit number. As if.

Remember this: *Cash is king*. Living within your means and relying on cash gives you a financial cushion that allows you to make life decisions without worrying about some arbitrary number that's supposed to dictate your choices. There's more than one way to skin a cat (a curious expression, but fitting here) — there's more than one way to achieve financial security. Don't get entrapped in the narrow mindset that a credit score is your only ticket to a financially secure life.

It's not.

12

---∞---

Navigating Taxes

When did you last sit down to organize your old school-work? Or do you throw them away? Well, you can now add your year-end financial documents to your pile (to organize, not throw away). It may seem tedious, but it's necessary. Year-end documents are a collection of financial records and statements that summarize your financial activities for the year. They're your financial history, proving what you've earned, spent, and saved.

Organizing these documents is as simple as creating a designated binder with dividers and labeled tabs. Make it a practice to store new documents as soon as you receive them. You'll need them for making major life decisions. You'll also need them for filing (dreaded) taxes.

Let's get one thing straight—you can't dodge taxes. Avoiding this responsibility will land you in hot water. You could end up facing penalties or even jail time. As the old saying goes, "Don't mess with the IRS."

Consider taxes as a membership fee for living in your country—only you can't opt out. They're the dues you pay to keep the government and its many services running, including education, transportation, housing, healthcare, energy, and agriculture. So, let's ensure you understand the basics and keep Uncle Sam happy and at bay.

The Tax Forms

When filing taxes, you'll need one of two forms: the W-2 or the 1099. These forms report your income to the IRS (Internal Revenue Service). If you earned your money through a traditional employer-employee setup, you'll use a W-2 (Jones, 2022), which your employer provides, typically by January 31st (Hoover, 2023). Your W-2 contains specific information about your income from the previous year. It summarizes your employment details, such as earnings, taxes withheld, and benefits received.

If you earned money through freelance gigs, you'll use a 1099 (Jones, 2022). Recall that as a self-employed freelancer, no one withholds or pays taxes throughout the year on your behalf, making it crucial to maintain detailed records of your completed projects for tax purposes. Now is the time to put those meticulous records to use and pay the taxes.

Electronic or Paper

There are two methods for filing taxes: electronic and paper. Uncle Sam doesn't care which method you use. If you're tech-savvy, numerous apps and websites are available for electronic filing, providing step-by-step guidance. Alternatively, if you prefer the traditional approach, you can find paper forms at your local library or post office.

Tax Refund or Bill

Once you've completed your tax filing, you'll either receive a tax refund or a bill. A tax refund is essentially the IRS saying, "Oops, we collected too much from your paychecks. Here's your change. And thanks for the loan." Getting a tax refund may feel like you've won a mini lottery. But no—it's *your* money the IRS is returning in overpaid taxes due to your employer withholding too much throughout the year. In contrast, if you end up with a tax bill, your employer didn't withhold enough, and now you'll owe the taxes and must pay the difference.

To avoid surprises, complete the W-4 accurately so that your withholding closely matches your tax obligation. Recall that the W-4 is one of those new-hire employment forms we discussed, which tells your employer the amount of money to withhold from your paychecks for taxes. So, whether you receive a refund or a bill, visit your HR department to update your W-4 and fine-tune your withholding amount for the current year. The goal is to aim for a tax balance as close to zero as possible, eliminating the likelihood of either a refund, which could have been invested for earnings, or a tax bill that may lead to stress as you scramble to cover the amount due.

If you find all this tax talk confusing, it's because taxes *are* confusing. It's like trying to solve a Rubik's Cube with your feet while blindfolded. Just know that if you earn money, you must pay taxes. Maintain records you think you'll need and use them to file your taxes by the deadline.

Here comes your third and final congratulations. Congratulations! Reaching teenager status—congrats. Opening a Roth IRA—congrats. Getting through taxes—congrats! You made it all the way. Sorry, I had to end it with taxes, but I couldn't *start* with taxes. You wouldn't have made it here.

"It's never too early to learn money skills."

Conclusion

Money Skills for Teens has equipped you with the essential tools to successfully navigate the world of personal finance. You possess the ability to educate yourself and take control of your financial well-being. Through books, blogs, videos, or podcasts, the opportunity to expand your financial literacy is at your fingertips.

It's easy to think, "I understand all of this, but it can wait." Remember, many adults now working ridiculously hard to stay financially afloat once had the same thought and wish they had acted sooner. Don't let this be you, please. I don't want you to learn money lessons the hard way. Time is a valuable asset—once gone, it's gone. And time is money. You've heard the saying. But now, it takes on a whole new meaning.

Look at success stories like Warren Buffet, who bought his first stock at age 11, marking the beginning of his long and successful career as an investor, or tech entrepreneurs who made their first million before graduating high school. Yes, they had talent and a genius gene, but they also had financial smarts—a whole lot of it. I'm not suggesting you compare yourself to them. Instead, use them as inspiration, apply the financial smarts you've gained here, and start making moves!

Set financial goals, no matter how small they may seem. Track your expenses to understand where your money goes. Create budgets and stick to them. Set up an emergency fund for unexpected costs and sinking funds for your aspirations. Open a Roth IRA and invest in index funds. Explore passive income streams when you're not busy. Stay out of debt. Pay your taxes. Connect with like-minded individuals. Wherever you are, the doorway to a bright future is wide open.

This book is in your hands because somebody thinks you have what it takes to shape a prosperous future filled with boundless opportunities. If you picked it up, all the more!

As you step across that doorway, embrace the ongoing journey, gain wisdom through experiences, and make every financial decision with purpose.

Destination: Retirement. *It starts with you and ends with you.*

Circling back to those three questions at the start of this book. Has this journey shifted your view of money, injected new life into your aspirations, and painted a more vibrant picture of the future you envision? *That's wisdom gained.*

Farewell, Friend.

Don't forget to share this with Bestie.

Thank You

Thanks for grabbing my book and making it to the end!

If you found value in this book, please consider sharing an honest review on Amazon. Your feedback guides others to discover the same value and helps me create books that align with your needs and interests.

Additionally, leaving a review is the simplest and most effective way to support independent authors like myself.

You can leave a review by scanning the QR Code or visiting the URL below.

I genuinely appreciate your consideration!

Kae

https://amazon.com/review/create-review

References

Ameriprise Investment Research Group. (2023, April 3). *Stock Market Performance After Bear Markets.* Ameriprise. https://tinyurl.com /3c2y2hxj

Barroso, A. (2023, June 29). *How to Calculate Your Credit Utilization Ratio.* NerdWallet. https://tinyurl.com/4rsbd5dw

Beers, B. (2023, June 5). *How and When Are Stock Dividends Paid Out?* Investopedia. https://tinyurl.com/499emedv

Bell, M. (2023, September 27). *Should You Use a Roth Account Even if You Prefer Traditional?* Sound Mind Investing. https://tinyurl.com /ys8bxadh

Bennett, K. (2023, October 3). *What Is Compound Interest?* Bankrate. https://tinyurl.com/428ncs59

Bloomenthal, A. (2023, September 28). *How to Invest in the S&P 500.* Investopedia. https://tinyurl.com/wp8unxay

Bowen, J. (2023, November 13). *Publicly Traded Companies: Definition and Examples.* The Motley Fool. https://tinyurl.com/2s3fnp5k

Brewster, L. (2023, March 7). *How to Invest in the S&P 500 and Get Exposure to the Biggest and Best American Companies.* Fortune. https:// tinyurl.com/274v97d9

Brock, C. (2023, May 15). *All About Asset Classes and Investment Diversification.* The Motley Fool. https://tinyurl.com/2s3fnp5k

Brock, C. (2023, May 17). *What Is a Credit Score: Definitions, Factors, and Ways to Raise It.* Investopedia. https://tinyurl.com/45jfpr46

Brock, C. (2023, November 16). *Saving vs. Investing: Which Route Should You Take?* The Motley Fool. https://tinyurl.com/yn8ha9cu

Burnette, M. (2022, March 18). *Checking vs. Savings Account: The Difference and How to Choose.* NerdWallet. https://tinyurl.com/2ekzf93w

Burns, P. (2023, August 15). *ETF vs. Index Fund.* Money. https://tinyurl.com/4666aae6

Camargo, M. (2023, May 23). *30 Investing Terms to Know.* Credit Karma. https://tinyurl.com/w6983fe9

Carey, R. (2023, December 5). *Vanguard vs. Fidelity: What's the Difference?* Unbiased. http://tinyurl.com/33j9zmx6

Coombes, A. (2023, November 23). *Can You Have a Roth IRA and a 401K?* NerdWallet. https://tinyurl.com/3b6effnf

Curry, B. (2021, September 30). *How Many Funds Do You Need in Your Retirement Accounts?* Forbes Advisor. https://tinyurl.com/3fusu5tf

Daly, L. (2023, August 8). *Here's Why You Should Invest Even When the Market Is Down.* The Motley Fool. https://tinyurl.com/42ur3c92

Dehan, A. (2023, January 6). *Capital Gains Tax for Roth IRAs.* SmartAsset. https://tinyurl.com/24573nj9

Depersio, G. (2023, May 16). *What Affects Your Credit Score?* Investopedia. https://tinyurl.com/4vfa2ues

DiLallo, M. (2023, September 26). *What Is Net Asset Value?* The Motley Fool. https://tinyurl.com/9s2n6jnn

Downey, L. (2023, October 20). *What Is a Freelancer: Examples, Taxes, Benefits, and Drawbacks.* Investopedia. https://tinyurl.com /bdz95ncm

Fernando, J. (2023, May 18). *The Power of Compound Interest: Calculations and Examples.* Investopedia. https://tinyurl.com/r8azh9nr

Fernando, J. (2023, May 24). *Return on Investment (ROI): How to Calculate It and What It Means.* Investopedia. https://tinyurl.com/33yh8fvc

Fernando, J. (2023, October 31). *Opportunity Cost: Definition, Calculation, Formula, and Examples.* Investopedia. https://tinyurl.com /46w855a3

Fernando, J. (2023, November 28). *What Is a 401(k) and How Does It Work?* Investopedia. https://tinyurl.com/26umrd6t

Fidelity. (n.d.). *Understanding How Mutual Funds, ETFs, and Stocks Trade.* https://tinyurl.com/42k6rpzp

Fidelity. (n.d.). *Why Diversification Matters.* https://tinyurl.com/jrbvwx73

Fishman, S. (n.d.). *The Ultimate Guide to Getting Your Freelance Taxes Right.* Collective. https://tinyurl.com/ypcz2zy5

Folger, J. (2023, April 30). *Brokerage Account vs. IRA: What's the Difference?* Investopedia. https://tinyurl.com/3pj7wm7w

Folger, J. (2023, July 16). *Should You Reinvest Dividends: A Practical Guide.* Time Stamped. https://tinyurl.com/56vwz3e4

Folger, J. (2023, November 3). *Opening a Roth IRA for Your Kids Offers Investment Options, Tax-Free Growth, and a Great Lesson in How to Save*. Business Insider. https://tinyurl.com/mfs4sw5c

Folger, J. (2023, November 20). *Roth IRA Withdrawal Rules*. Investopedia. https://tinyurl.com/bdd847t5

Fontinelle, E. (2023, September 29). *4 Basic Things to Know about Bonds*. Investopedia. https://tinyurl.com/y84bn3sw

Frankel, M. (2023, November 17). *What Is Compound Interest?* The Motley Fool. https://tinyurl.com/2d6wspmb

Goldberg, M. (2023, May 2). *FDIC Insurance: What It Is and How It Works*. Bankrate. https://tinyurl.com/yy7s6chp

Gravler, E. (2023, April 21). *Index Funds Are One of the Easiest Ways to Invest – Here's How They Work*. CNBC. https://tinyurl.com/y4vefbav

Haegele, B. (2023, September 6). *Switching Online Brokers: Here's How to Transfer Your Investments to a New Account*. Bankrate. https://tinyurl.com/2s3dp86a

Hartill, R. (2022, November 29). *When Did the Roth IRA Start?* The Balance. https://tinyurl.com/scsu3kv8

Hayes, A. (2023, April 26). *Dollar-Cost Averaging (DCA) Explained With Examples and Considerations*. Investopedia. https://tinyurl.com/2ty2m93b

Hayes, A. (2023, September 15). *Trade Definition in Finance: Benefits and How It Works*. Investopedia. https://tinyurl.com/y9xx4vfm

Herrity, J. (2023, July 10). *How to Write SMART Goals in 5 Steps (With Examples)*. Indeed. https://tinyurl.com/2ryk5m4t

Heyford, S. (2023, July 16). *Rebalance Your Portfolio to Stay on Track.* Investopedia. https://tinyurl.com/35accutk

Hoover, L. (2023, January 11). *4 Steps to Take if You Don't Receive Your W-2.* PrimePay. https://tinyurl.com/bdd4vt7j

Investor.gov. (n.d.). *Financial Tools and Calculators: Compound Interest Calculator.* U.S. Securities and Exchange Committee. https://tinyurl.com/ytkx3hnb

IRS.gov. (2023, August 29). *Operating a 401(k) Plan.* https://tinyurl.com/ms9rcsmn

IRS.gov. (2023, October 17). *Topic No. 409, Capital Gains and Losses.* https://tinyurl.com/9dbwk6ux

Jones, J. (2022, April 20). *1099 vs. W-2 Employee: What Is the Difference?* LendingTree. https://tinyurl.com/5ewv24sd

Josephson, A. (2023, July 30). *Federal Income Tax Brackets for the Tax Year 2023.* SmartAsset. https://tinyurl.com/yp9cfk5j

Kennon, J. (2022, January 26). *Why Do Stock Prices Fluctuate?* The Balance. https://tinyurl.com/3nz6vswd

Kindness, D. (2023, November 7). *Roth IRA vs. Traditional IRA: Key Differences.* Investopedia. https://tinyurl.com/mt6cn69x

Kumok, Z. (2023, November 19). *How to Invest at Every Age.* Investopedia. https://tinyurl.com/ycxcvnsx

Lake, R. (2023, January 13). *How to Build a Three-Fund Portfolio.* SmartAsset. https://tinyurl.com/45zf59k9

Lake, R. (2023, April 13). *70/30 vs. 80/20 Asset Allocation: Which Is Better?* SmartAsset. https://tinyurl.com/4kyhtdhd

Levy, A. (2023, November 21). *3 Reasons to Invest in Index Funds.* The Motley Fool. https://tinyurl.com/5n7ksvwr

Loudenback, T. (2020, May 23). *When You're Investing for the Long-Term, Experts Say There's No 'Bad' Time to Get into the Market.* Business Insider. https://tinyurl.com/4j4vnmpk

Martinez, J. (2023, July 28). *How to Read a Bank Statement and Actually Understand It.* DocuClipper. https://tinyurl.com/5ffkcudd

Maverick, J. (2023, May 24). *S&P 500 Average Return.* Investopedia. https://tinyurl.com/5yvdhkmu

O'Shea, A. (2023, September 12). *Roth IRA Withdrawal Rules: What You Need to Know.* NerdWallet. https://tinyurl.com/why7zxs8

O'Shea, A. (2023, November 21). *What Is a Brokerage Account and How Do I Open One?* NerdWallet. https://tinyurl.com/y6x8hv5u

Prinzel, Y. (2023, September 10). *401(k) vs. IRA: What's the Difference?* Investopedia. https://tinyurl.com/mr2vwxys

Quotes on Finance. (n.d.). *Financial Quotes from Albert Einstein.* https://tinyurl.com/49rbcepv

Rather, S. (2023, May 3). *What Happens if You Go Over Your Credit Card Limit?* NerdWallet. https://tinyurl.com/27u3pyxm

Rosenberg, E. (2023, November 23). *Best Student Checking Accounts for November 2023*. Time Stamped. https://tinyurl.com/2re3kdb7

Royal, J. (2023, June 16). *Why Is Portfolio Diversification Important for Investors?* Bankrate. https://tinyurl.com/5eythnua

Royal, J. (2023, July 20). *What Is Drip Investing: Learn How to Compound Your Wealth.* Bankrate. https://tinyurl.com/58cekypc

Schwahn, L. (2022, November 10). *Zero-Based Budgeting: Spend Every Penny but Meet Your Financial Goals.* NerdWallet. https://tinyurl.com/mr3ajps7

Scott, M. (2023, November 7). *Backdoor Roth IRA: Advantages and Tax Implications Explained.* Investopedia. https://tnyurl.com/mrxvkjt7

Shultz, M. (2023, November 17). *Average Credit Card Interest Rate in America Today.* Lendingtree. https://tinyurl.com/4c8xesr9

Sinusoid, D. (2021, September 4). *J.L. Collins: How to Balance Your Investment Portfolio.* Shortform. https://tinyurl.com/4zckbf45

Smith, L. (2023, November 13). *Bank ATM Fees: How Much Are They and How Can You Avoid Them?* SmartAsset. https://tinyurl.com/4h49e4ap

Speights, K. (2023, September 10). *Here's How Warren Buffett's Favorite Index Fund Could Help Make You a Millionaire.* The Motley Fool. https://tinyurl.com/5h2xumxd

Stevens, T. (2023, February 10). *What's the Difference Between a Bank and a Credit Union?* Forbes Advisor. https://tinyurl.com/35wda4vw

Success With Money. (2023). *Total Stock Market Index Fund or S&P 500 Index Fund.* https://tinyurl.com/44e64f6h

Swenson, S. (2023, November 9). *What Is a Custodial Roth IRA?* The Motley Fool. https://tinyurl.com/3c3z2a23

Tarpley, L. G. (2023, July 12). *How Much You Should Have in Savings at Every Age.* Business Insider. https://tinyurl.com/4r8kmm3p

Taylor, K. (2023, October 23). *How Old Do You Have to Be to Get a Credit Card?* Bankrate. https://tinyurl.com/hn4teuxb

Thune, K. (2022, October 17). *Total Stock Market vs. S&P 500 Index.* The Balance. https://tinyurl.com/mr2m8fdm

Tretina, K. (2023, March 15). *Stocks vs. Bonds: Know the Difference.* Forbes Advisor. https://tinyurl.com/3w4e8kpz

Tretina, K. (2023, March 22). *Index Funds vs. Mutual Funds.* Forbes Advisor. https://tinyurl.com/3xrkczyn

Tretina, K. (2023, November 3). *Vanguard vs. Fidelity: Which Is Better?* U.S. News. https://tinyurl.com/yab9n8tm

Tretina, K. (2023, November 7). *What Is a 401(k) Match?* Forbes Advisor. https://tinyurl.com/4zn95mzx

Vanguard. (n.d.). *ETFs. vs. Mutual Funds: A Comparison.* https://tinyurl.com/4xs86b3u

Walrack, J. (2022, May 30). *Should You Open Your Roth IRA at Your Bank?* The Balance. https://tinyurl.com/3bs2f869

Walrack, J. (2022, September 16). *How to Budget for Taxes as a Freelancer and Avoid an Expensive Tax Bill.* U.S. News. https://tinyurl.com/5dv5x9cp

Walrack, J. (2023, October 20). *Typical Minimum Balance for Traditional Savings Accounts.* The Balance. https://tinyurl.com/wc9p6869

Ward, J. (2023, February 3.). *Reasons Why You Should Aim to Save 15% for Retirement.* T. Rowe Price. https://tinyurl.com/y5ahwce3

Waterworth, K. (2023, April 19). *What Is a Stock Ticker?* The Motley Fool. https://tinyurl.com/5f4z3cww

White, T. (2022, May 19). *It's Time in the Market, Not Timing the Market.* Bestinvest. https://tinyurl.com/4nsuh4df

Yochim, D. (2023, July 14). *Index Funds vs. Mutual Funds: The Differences That Matter.* NerdWallet. https://tinyurl.com/29jwe7kj

Yochim, D. (2023, November 1). *How to Invest in Index Funds and Best Index Funds of November.* NerdWallet. https://tinyurl.com/22d6d6d8

Made in United States
Troutdale, OR
05/13/2024

19837781R00116